P9-CRD-544

THE KU KLUX KLAN

AMERICA'S RECURRING NIGHTMARE

The Ku Klux Klan: America's Recurring Nightmare

FRED J. COOK

Julian Messner

Published by Julian Messner, a division of Silver Burdett Press, Inc.,
Simon & Schuster, Inc., Prentice Hall Bldg., Englewood Cliffs, NJ 07632

JULIAN MESSNER and colophon are trademarks of Simon & Schuster, Inc.
Manufactured in the United States of America.
Design by Elaine Groh

Lib. ed. 10 9 8 7 6 5 4 3 2 1

Library of Congress Cataloging-in-Publication Data

Cook, Fred J.
The Ku Klux Klan: America's recurring nightmare.

Bibliography: p. 143
Includes index.
Summary: Explores the consistent pattern of racial bigotry, religious intolerance, violence, and exploitation by the Klan since its founding in the post-Civil War period.
1. Ku Klux Klan—Juvenile literature.
2. Ku Klux Klan (1915-   )—Juvenile literature.
3. Racism—United States—History—Juvenile literature
4. United States—Race relations—Juvenile literature.
[1. Ku Klux Klan. 2. Racism. 3. Race relations]
I. Title
E668.C77   1989   322.4′2′0973   89-8265
ISBN 0-671-68421-3

CONTENTS

CHAPTER

1

THE KLAN LIVES ON

THE Ku Klux Klan never dies. For more than a century, it has peddled doctrines of racial hate with such effect that the supposedly civilized 1980s have been marked by explosions of violence: the desecration of synagogues, the burning of black homes, beatings, stabbings, murder. All in the name of 100 percent Americanism.

Some of these atrocities have been committed by the Klan; others by its imitators and followers in the hate brigade—by youthful neo-Nazi Skinheads who parade regularly with the Klan; by older neo-Nazi groups, many led by Klansmen, who train with military weapons and plot the overthrow of the government.

Whatever the group, the message is the Klan's message. The battle cry is "White power! White power!" And the racial viciousness is reflected in their shouts that those they dislike are apes.

While blacks and Jews are principal targets of the Klan, and have been for generations, they are not alone. Hate has been directed, too, at civil rights workers, labor organizers, and all foreigners, especially Hispanics and Vietnamese.

Klansmen in their peaked white hoods and flowing white robes have paraded the streets of America ever since the post–Civil War period. At times, as their movement flourished, they have marched by the thousands; at others, in thin, scraggly lines. Whatever the circumstances of the moment, the hate-filled message lives on.

The original Klan was formed in the South right after the Civil War. Its purpose: to control the newly enfranchised black voters and the northern ward politicians (Carpetbaggers, they were called) who had taken control of the conquered states of the Confederacy.

When the Reconstruction Era ended in the South in 1877, the Carpetbaggers departed and the Klan faded away. But it left behind a myth of knight-errantry that has been used time and again by cheap opportunists to revive the Klan for the benefit of their own pocketbooks.

One of these revivals occurred in the 1920s when the Klan movement swept the nation, dominating politics in several states. It appealed then to three basic prejudices: Klansmen were anti-black, anti-Semitic and anti-Catholic. Catholics were especially targeted; they were portrayed as threatening to seize the national government, with the Pope tunneling his way into the White House.

This movement crested, then subsided as American common sense reasserted itself. Like an ebb tide in the ocean, the Klan receded, only to be reborn in all its viciousness during the integration and civil rights struggles of the 1960s and 1970s. There was, however, one notable change. Anti-Catholicism was shelved. The Klan now perceived Catholics as allies against creeping communism.

Federal prosecutions of Klan leaders who had been involved in some of the most vicious deeds resulted in a number of convictions and jail sentences. The Klan movement was temporarily crippled, but a number of separate Klans continued to peddle the same messages of bigotry and hate.

They peddled them in Forsyth County, Georgia. The Klan had driven blacks and Hispanics out of Forsyth. Only one black person lived in a county of 35,600 people. At one time a sign was erected warning blacks who worked in Forsyth: "Niggers, don't let the sun set on you in Forsyth."

In 1987, some white citizens rebelled against this ingrained racism. They called for a brotherhood march on Martin Luther King Jr. Day, January 17. They were joined by busloads of whites and blacks from Atlanta. The buses were met by a mob of local racists, led by Klansmen in full regalia carrying the Confederate flag. "It was a lynch mob," one marcher said. "We didn't even get off the bus when two bottles came through the window."

The Klan-led mob swelled to 1,000. They screamed obscenities and racial epithets, brandished fists and clubs, hurled rocks and bottles. Skeleton police forces were overwhelmed; the march had to be abandoned. But some national TV newscasts broadcast the riotous scene, and there was a widespread backlash against the Klan.

The Center for Democratic Renewal in Atlanta and allied civil rights groups organized a second brotherhood march a week later, January 24. An estimated 20,000 people from various sections of the nation marshalled for a march on the Forsyth County Courthouse. The Klan, backed by members from other states, rallied a force of some 2,000, many armed with chains, knives and even bows and arrows. Violence erupted along the line of march, but this time National Guardsmen and officers of the Georgia Bureau of Investigation were there to protect the demonstrators. Some sixty racists were arrested, and the mighty river of 20,000 marchers flowed on. They reached the courthouse, where speakers denounced the Klan and racism. Overwhelmed by the odds, one Klansman shouted: "Boys, we've lost this country. That's it."

There was, however, a sequel. That night, a church in Forsyth County was burned to the ground. It had once had a few blacks in its congregation.

A significant aspect of the Forsyth County riots was the large number of youths among the most violent racists. This was not unusual. During the 1970s and early 1980s, Klan leaders had launched campaigns to recruit youths, bombarding many schools with hate-filled literature. Some tracts denied that the Holocaust (the slaughtering of six million Jews in Nazi gas chambers in World War II) had ever happened; others fantasized a great Jewish-communist conspiracy.

This indoctrination of youth apparently had its effect, for the 1980s have seen the birth of a violent Skinhead movement. The Skinheads are youths in their teens or early twenties who shave the hair off the sides of their heads, wear leather jackets and heavy leather boots, and often tattoo their arms with swastikas.

Skinheads originated in Great Britain as punk rock followers. Some in this country still are. But by far the most prominent are Skinheads who have adopted a neo-Nazi philosophy and who, according to the Anti-Defamation League of B'nai B'rith, have paraded in every major rally hed by the old-line Klans.

These militant Skinheads have a penchant for raw violence. One nineteen-year-old Detroit Skinhead summarized his thinking this way: "What makes a Skinhead? Attitude. White power. 'Cause Niggers suck. Niggers and Jews. They're half monkeys. They should all be killed."

Such hate-dominated youths sometimes commit murder:

- Two Skinhead brothers, one eighteen, the other sixteen, were arrested in Florida for the stabbing death of a black man outside the Tampa Museum of Art on December 20, 1987.

- In San Jose, California, Skinhead Michel Elrod pleaded guilty to killing a local rock musician who had tried to keep him from stabbing a black man at a party on February 28, 1988. Elrod allegedly had shouted, "Let's go get the nigger." And when the musician intervened, Elrod stabbed him instead.

- In Portland, Oregon, in November, two friends let an Ethiopian out of the car at his door. He was set upon by a gang of Skinheads and beaten to death with a baseball bat. His friends were also beaten. Police arrested three Skinhead youths for the murder.

As shocking as the murders was the crucifixion torture of Greg Withrow in Sacramento, California. Withrow had headed the Aryan Youth Movement, named after its parent, White Aryan Resistance, a neo-Nazi organization that advocates forming a separate white nation out of five states in the Pacific Northwest. Withrow had been one of the most frenzied youth orators, calling for violence and genocide. Then he fell in love with a woman named Sylvia, and love conquered hate.

Withrow resigned from Aryan Youth. In early July, 1988, he said, his former followers, accusing him of treason, invaded his apartment and beat him with baseball bats. They warned him not to talk. They followed up the warning with a grisly demonstration. On August 9 they captured Withrow, spread-eagled him on an eight-foot-wide board crucifixion style and drove nails through his hands, as he said, "real slow."

Withrow was succeeded as president of Aryan Youth by John Metzger, the son of White Aryan Resistance leader Tom Metzger. The elder Metzger, forty-five, a TV repairman, had been California Grand Dragon of the Knights of the Ku Klux Klan. In 1980, he captured the Democratic nomination for Congress in San Diego, polling 40,000 votes. Defeated by his Republican opponent in the general election, he soon emerged as head of White Aryan Resistance.

In his new role, he began videotaping interviews with racist leaders for a cable television program he called "Race and Reason." The telecast was seen in more than twenty-five cities in a dozen states. One Skinhead interviewed on the program said, "We should start gassing all these niggers and get rid of them because there's no need to keep paying taxes on their worthless lives."

John Metzer, who had succeeded Withrow as leader of the Skinheads, often appeared with his father on "Race and Reason," and in November, 1988, he came to New York City for an appearance on a Geraldo Rivera TV show titled "Young Hate Mongers."

The show was put together following a Skinhead attack in the New York subway. William Stump, thirty-one, of Bayonne, New Jersey, was waiting with his wife and three-year-old daughter for a PATH train to New Jersey when four Skinheads burst onto the platform. A Port Authority policeman said they were shouting "racial hatred muck against blacks and Hispanics and anyone else they could think of."

Stump resented their neo-Nazi rhetoric and told them to "knock it off." A fight followed. The Skinheads began to beat Stump, and one of them seized the baby's stroller and was about to pitch it and the child down a flight of stairs when Stump jabbed a lighted cigarette into the Skinhead's face. One of the other Skinheads smashed Stump in the side of his head with a bottle, fracturing his cheekbones. Port Authority police rescued Stump and arrested the four Skinheads, who ranged in age from seventeen to twenty-three.

The Rivera "Young Hate Mongers" program followed on November 3, 1988. Rivera, who is always looking for confrontational subjects, set up a program featuring John Metzger; Bob Heick, of Racist American Fronts; and Michael Palasch, of the National White Resistance. Confronting them were Roy Innis, head of the Congress of Racial Equality, and Rabbi A. Bruce Goldman, of the Center for Creative Jewish Living.

The program began with Rivera reading some of the more violent Skinhead statements. The Skinheads were slow to explain their thinking, and a woman in the audience asked Metzger why he didn't answer questions. "I'm tired of listening to kikes and this Uncle Tom here," Metzger replied, referring to Innis.

Innis, always combative on racial issues, rose to his feet, confronted the Skinheads and doubled his fist at them in mock aggression.

Metzger tried to rise, and Innis grabbed him by the throat. As the two briefly tussled, Heick threw a chair at Rivera and a wild melee erupted. Skinheads in the audience joined those on the show; some twenty persons swung punches, shouted, wrestled. Rivera came out of the fracas with blood all over his face, his nose broken.

This miniature riot on national television exposed the violence-prone, hate-filled young racists to a wide audience. They have been compared by some experts—and, indeed, they often see themselves—as storm troopers, the modern advance guard of racism. Skinheads have served as bodyguards for Klan officials; they have marched shoulder to shoulder in Klan and neo-Nazi demonstrations; they have assaulted and harassed minority students in colleges; they have defaced synagogues.

Their ranks are composed of the rebellious and disillusioned. Many come from broken homes. Most come from poor or submerged lower-middle-class families. They feel locked out of the benefits of the economic system and rebel against the establishment. And so they are receptive to the Klan's messages of hate.

The Anti-Defamation League of B'nai B'rith reported that Skinheads were largely responsible for the 17 percent increase in anti-Semitic crimes in 1987. And the record for 1988 was even worse. Anti-Semitic incidents in the nation rose to a five-year high in 1988, with Skinheads thought to be responsible for forty-one major incidents in fifteen states. The league reported a 41 percent increase in anti-Semitic harassment and an 18.5 percent increase in vandalism. This included swastika daubings, arson, and even the fire bombings of some synagogues.

Hate-inspired racial incidents reported by legal authorities totaled nearly 1,300 in forty states, the District of Columbia, and Puerto Rico, the report said. Authors of the report commented that it seemed ironic that, even as the Klan itself was weakening, violence was growing. They attributed this in large measure to the Klan's success in indoctrinating youth. The Skinhead movement resulted, and it is growing—from 1,500 in twelve states in February 1988, to 2,000 in twenty states in October.

These are only the youthful recruits of racism. Law enforcement officials estimate that between 15,000 and 20,000 persons belong to hate groups such as the White Aryan Resistance and the Ku Klux Klan. But this is only the fraction of the hate brigade that surfaces. The virus of bigotry and hate runs much deeper, as Tom Metzger's 40,000 votes at the polls demonstrated.

The question remains: How did a country that historically has been a melting pot for diverse races, a country founded on beliefs of freedom of speech and freedom of religion for all, ever come to nurture such frenzies of hate and violence? The answer lies in more than a century of passionate appeals to prejudice by the Ku Klux Klan. Here, then, is the record of America's oldest and most persistent hate-mongering organization.

CHAPTER 2

AN ACCIDENTAL BIRTH

It was Christmas Eve, 1865, in the small, poverty-stricken town of Pulaski, Tennessee. The South had just lost the Civil War. Desolation and despair hung like a pall over the states of the conquered Confederacy. The Christmas season in this year of defeat and disaster was not a happy one.

Six young Confederate veterans, penniless and with prospects as grim as those of their ravaged land, sat around a stove in a law office located in a small brick building. Their spirits were at lowest ebb. Something was definitely needed to jar them out of their mood of depression and bring some spirit back into their lives.

"Boys," one of them said, "let's start something to break the monotony and cheer up our mothers and girls. Let's start a club of some kind."

Almost any idea that promised a diversion would have been welcomed by that small group on this saddest of Christmas Eves, and so it was agreed that they would meet again soon and try to get their club organized.

The second meeting was held shortly afterward at the home of a prominent citizen of Pulaski, Colonel Thomas Martin. The young men's first problem was to choose a name for their club. One suggested "Kuklio," from the Greek word meaning a band or circle. Since all were of Scotch-Irish descent, another suggested adding the word "Klan." Ideas were tossed back and forth; and as their thoughts seemed to be running to *K's*, someone suggested "Ku." Putting it all together, the group came up with the name that was to live in American history for more than a century, right down to the present time—Ku Klux Klan.

The founders were bent simply on merrymaking, on any kind of prank that would banish the gloom of the times and lift spirits. Because masquerades were very popular, it occurred to them that they should garb themselves in some outlandish costumes. And so they raided the linen closet.

There all they found were some stiff linen sheets and pillow cases. Materials for fancy costumes were not available in the war-impoverished South, and so they decided the linen sheets and pillow cases would have to do. They would cover their heads with the pillow cases, drape themselves in the sheets, and ride out to serenade their parents and sweethearts. And while they were about it, they decided, they might as well drape their horses in linen sheets, too; they would add to the show.

So it was that the Ku Klux Klan took to the road for the first time. Its original members formed a small band that rode across the countryside, visiting from house to house amid much surprise and frolicking. The six young men who had conceived the idea certainly achieved their original purpose—and much more besides.

To understand the unexpected impact these merry pranksters had upon their time, one has to appreciate the dismal situation of the postwar South. For the trampled states of the Confederacy, the Civil War did not really end with the surrender of General Robert E. Lee at

Appomattox in 1865. It was to continue in guerrilla fashion for another twenty-two years.

Had Abraham Lincoln lived, this tragedy might have been avoided, but the wartime President, who had freed the slaves, had been assassinated. Lincoln's whole purpose had been to preserve the Union and, with victory, to heal the wounds of war and bind the Union together again. He and his successor, Andrew Johnson, had been willing to accept the good-faith pledges of loyalty given by the Confederate generals and statesmen who had led the revolt—and to place the government of the southern states in their hands. But everything changed in the South when Congress took over Reconstruction. Controlled by Republican radicals, Congress rebelled at the idea of treating the leaders of the conquered South as equals. It divided the conquered land into military districts. The northern army was sent in and quartered in strategic cities; and it was followed by a horde of scavengers.

The former white leaders in the South were now disenfranchised; they were barred from the practice of law. Unable to vote, unable in most states to defend themselves in court, they were shoved ruthlessly aside while a new Radical coalition seized control of every branch of government.

This coalition was composed of some unscrupulous Southerners—called derisively Scalawags—and adventurers from the North who came with their life's possessions in carpetbags. These Carpetbaggers were a mixture of the lowest type of ward politicians, soldiers of fortune, and even some degenerates. "We are in the hands of camp followers, horse-holders, crooks, bottle-washers, and thieves," declared General J. H. Clanton, a reputable citizen of Alabama. The result was "a real reign of terror...among the whites."

The Carpetbaggers recruited their following among the recently freed blacks. These people were uneducated and credulous because, before the war, it had been a crime in the South to teach a black to read and write. Hence, they formed an ideal audience for the oratory of the Scalawag-Carpetbagger politicians. By such measures, the world of the South was turned upside down.

The blacks on the southern plantations had been traditionally a docile people. Southern white masters in the prewar slavery period had always been haunted by fears of black uprisings and the rape of their women. These fears, stemming from their own hidden guilt, had been in the main unjustified. Except for rare, quickly suppressed outbreaks, the slaves had remained quiet and obedient. Even during the war, though their white masters were absent on the battlefields and white women had been left unprotected, the blacks had not risen in revolt, and women had rarely been harmed. Now the Scalawags and Carpetbaggers armed their black followers, forming them into militia bands to support their political rule. Blacks paraded with guns on their shoulders, a sight that frightened many whites.

Such was the land of the South when the Pulaski pranksters made their first rides. They soon noticed that their white-garbed apparitions were having a strange effect. Many people believed they were being haunted by ghosts when they saw white-robed men and white-covered horses riding at them out of the night.

The Klansmen were quick to play upon these fears, quick to see how the terror they inspired could be used to put their society back to what it had been. What had begun as a social prank turned into serious political action. The growing bands of Klansmen rode out deliberately to break up Carpetbagger political rallies and to chase and haunt those who attended them.

Sometimes a ghostly night rider would appear before the hut of a black follower of the Carpetbaggers. The visitor would stop his horse and ask for water. He would have thoughtfully provided himself with a rubber sack hidden under his robe. As the black man stared, the rider would thankfully "drink" three bucketfuls of water, remarking that he had traveled a thousand miles in the last twenty-four hours. "And," he would add, "that's the best water I have had since I was killed at the Battle of Shiloh."

As a final grisly touch he might stretch out a hand from beneath the white robe and show his black host a human skull. Usually the frightened man turned and fled.

Such visitations, repeated on an ever vaster scale, played on people's imaginations until the wildest tales circulated. White figures were reported sailing in the skies on white-clad horses above the roofs of towns. Their leader was always a superhumanly terrible figure—"ten feet high, his horse fifteen." He carried "a lance and a shield." Could anyone escape his vengence? Not a chance. These sky-riding spirits would pursue an enemy wherever he went, and he would be snatched away never to be seen again.

Local newspapers published chilling "general orders," supposedly issued by the spectral commander. They read:

"Shrouded Brotherhood! Murdered Heroes!

"Fling the bloody shirt that covers you to the four winds...Strike with the red-hot spear...The skies shall be blackened. A single Star shall look down upon horrible deeds. The night owl shall hoot a requiem over ghostly corpses..."

There was little wonder that black southerners, barraged by such propaganda, became fearful. Little wonder either that the Pulaski Klan grew like magic. Within three months, it had burst out of its original quarters and acquired a new headquarters on the edge of town. The building had been half-demolished in a cyclone. It was located on the side of a hill, its grounds cluttered with the shivered trunks of fallen trees.

It was a spectral-looking headquarters befitting the spectral riders who emerged from it to ride the country lanes at night, striking terror in the hearts of those who saw them. So started the Klan. Word of its activities and the effect it was having spread like wildfire through the South—and brought to Pulaski a Confederate hero whose name and ability were to make the Klan a regional force.

CHAPTER

3

FORREST TAKES COMMAND

THE armies of the Confederacy produced few leaders greater than Nathan Bedford Forrest. Robert E. Lee and Stonewall Jackson were the great heroes of the Army of Northern Virginia, but in Mississippi and Tennessee Forrest and his hard-riding "critter company" caused such havoc that Union commanders felt there could be no peace "until that devil Forrest is dead."

Forrest was not a West Pointer, but a self-made Mississippi plantation owner. Hence, he did not belong to the select group of professional soldiers who shared command of the Southern armies. Not until he had outwitted and outfought superior Union forces by his tactic of getting there "fustest with the mostest" were his talents recognized by the Confederate government. After he had been compelled to serve most of the war under superiors of indifferent talents, the Confederate government finally recognized his ability and promoted him to lieutenant general. But by then it was far too late to change the course of the war in the West, and historians were left to wonder what might have happened had Forrest been elevated to high command earlier.

After the war, Forrest returned to Mississippi and began the task of restoring his plantation. A powerfully built man, he possessed a sometimes fiery temper and so was easily aroused by the injustices he saw being inflicted on the South by the Scalawag-Carpetbagger regimes.

In May, 1866, he learned about the Klan movement that had been started in Pulaski. Forrest saw at once the possibility of using the Klan as a secret counterforce against the Union armies of occupation and their scoundrelly political allies. Eager to learn more about this new organization, he hurried to Nashville to see Captain John Morton, who had been his chief of artillery during the war.

Captain Morton had an office diagonally across the street from the Maxwell House, where Forrest lodged. Looking out his window one morning, he saw his former commander striding impatiently around the corner and hurried downstairs and out the door to meet him.

"John," Forrest said, "I hear this Ku Klux Klan is organized in Nashville, and I know you are in it. I want to join."

Morton dodged a direct answer and suggested they take a ride. Forrest kept pestering him with questions as they rode from the city out into the countryside, and Morton just kept smiling and changing the subject. Finally, having reached a lonely spot in dense woods outside the city, Morton stopped the buggy in which they were riding, turned to Forrest and said, "General, do you say you want to join the Ku Klux Klan?"

Thoroughly vexed by this time, Forrest uttered a few oaths and answered hotly, "Didn't I tell you that's what I came up here for?"

"Well, get out of the buggy, general," Morton said.

A bit bewildered, Forrest obeyed.

"Hold up your right hand," Morton told him.

Forrest raised his hand, and his former aide administered the preliminary oath of the order. As he finished taking the oath, Forrest said, "John, that's the worst swearing I ever did."

"That's all I can give you now," Morton told him. "Go to Room Number 10 at the Maxwell House tonight and you can get all you want. Now you know how to get in."

Such was the beginning of Nathan Bedford Forrest's association with the Klan. He and the other Klan leaders with whom he met at the Maxwell House realized that if their movement was to be effective, it must have a sound, closely knit organization. Separate Klaverns, as the local groups were called, could not be allowed to spring up all over the South and go their own ways without direction. A leader, a commander, was needed, and it was natural that the first man proposed for this role was General Robert E. Lee.

A delegation went to Virginia and appealed to General Lee to lead the movement. He refused because he was in poor health, but he wrote a letter saying that he approved of the Klan, although his backing must be "invisible." The committee then told him that, if he would not lead, General Forrest was their next choice.

"There is no man in the South who can handle so large a body of men so successfully," General Lee said. "Will you pay my respects to the general and tell him I hope he will succeed?"

Another meeting was held in Room Number 10 at the Maxwell House. Lee's letter was read and discussed. The word "invisible" in Lee's message struck a chord, and someone suggested that the Ku Klux Klan be called "the Invisible Empire," a title that has lasted to the present day. Next, the discussion focused on the commander and his title. Someone called out, "The Wizard of the Saddle, General Nathan Bedford Forrest." Forrest was immediately elected and installed as "the Grand Wizard of the Invisible Empire." He was given virtually dictatorial powers to run the Klan.

Forrest's rules were strict. Only veterans who had been honorably discharged or had been in Union prisons at war's end were eligible for membership in the Klan. Despite this limitation, Forrest soon commanded a secret army composed of 100,000 men spread throughout the states of the old Confederacy. Forrest became, in effect, the last ruler of the Old South.

He was admirably suited to the role. A will-o'-the-wisp in war, striking suddenly, fading away, riding hard to surprise and strike again, he was a master of ways that were secret, baffling, and mysterious—qualities that were essential if the Klan was to succeed.

Forrest's secret legions, it must be remembered, were in the position of the conquered challenging their conquerors. They were operating in defiance of Northern soldiers sent south to keep them in subjection, in defiance of Carpetbagger politicos and their militia, in defiance of Reconstruction judges intent on punishing the "rebels."

Forrest's wiliness was perhaps best illustrated by his maneuvering of a grand parade of the Klan on the streets of Pulaski on July 4, 1867. The way was prepared by the distribution on the sidewalks of printed slips of paper reading: "The Ku Klux Klan will parade the streets tonight."

This advance notice drew a large crowd into town from the surrounding countryside. Members of the Klan left their homes in late afternoon and traveled alone or in small groups to their rendezvous points, their white paraphernalia carefully concealed. If they were stopped and questioned, they merely said that they were going to Pulaski to watch the parade.

After nightfall, the riders assembled at designated points on the four roads leading into town. A skyrocket sent up from the middle of the town was the signal for them to mount and move. An eyewitness account describes what happened:

"The different companies met and joined each other on the Public Square in perfect silence; the discipline was admirable. Not a word was spoken. Necessary orders were given by means of whistles. In single file, in death-like stillness, they marched and countermarched throughout the town. While one column was headed north on one street, it was going south on the other. By crossing over in opposite directions the lines were kept in almost unbroken continuity. This marching and countermarching were kept up for about two hours, and the Klansmen departed as noiselessly as they came. The public was ever more mystified...

"Perhaps the greatest illusion produced was in regard to the numbers taking part in the parade. Reputable citizens were confident that the number was not less than three thousand. Others, whose imaginations were most easily wrought upon, were quite certain there were ten thousand. The truth is that the number of Ku Klux in the parade did not exceed four hundred."

Such demonstrations drove the rapscallion leaders of Reconstruction in the South almost crazy. They were frantic to learn the identity of the Klansmen and their leaders, but so secretive was the Klan, so ironbound its oath, that all their efforts were frustrated. Eventually, Forrest was suspected and was summoned to appear before a congressional investigating committee in Washington.

Here again the veteran cavalryman who believed in getting there "fustest with the mostest" demonstrated that the best defense lies in attack. Before his inquisitors could ask him a question, Forrest said, "It has been said that I was instrumental in getting the Klan up."

This was a statement that he could demolish with a ringing and truthful "No."

Asked by hostile congressmen and senators why the Klan had been created, Forrest testified that it resulted from the "insecurity felt by Southern people...Many Northern men [were] coming down there, forming Leagues all over the country. The Negroes were holding night meetings; were going about; were becoming very insolent; and the Southern people...were very much alarmed...Parties organized themselves so as to be ready if they were attacked. Ladies were ravished by some of those Negroes...There was a great deal of insecurity...This organization was got up to protect the weak, with no political intention at all..."

Forrest's description of Southern conditions was vivid, but he was not completely frank in describing the purpose of the Klan. True, the Klan's primary function was protection, but protection in the end involved political action. Only if the Scalawag-Carpetbagger forces could be overthrown could the old order of the South be restored.

CHAPTER

4

THE SECRET WAR

THE years from 1867 to 1870 saw a secret and sometimes vicious war being waged for political control of the South. On one side were the Scalawag-Carpetbagger forces, backed by their own militia and the votes of recently freed blacks; on the other, the white-robed Klansmen, led originally by officers who had been in the ranks of the Confederate army.

At first, the Klan used threats to scare blacks and keep them from voting, but as time went on and the struggle for control became more bitter, threats gave way to violence. Even some of the Klansmen admitted that they were "a rough bunch of boys."

Disgraceful scenes that marked Carpetbagger rule during the Reconstruction period fanned the fires of white disgust and hatred. In Louisiana, the Carpetbagger legislature of 1868 was a grubby, graft-hungry lot. As one historian wrote, legislative sessions were the scene of "dice games, drunken vomiting, and pitching shoes at the crystal chandeliers."

In North Carolina, there were similar scenes. A bar was opened in a little room at the top of the stairs in the State House, and legislators imbibed so freely that their chambers were often the scenes of drunken orgies. During one memorable session, two leaders presided in turn, one relieving the other as they made trips back and forth to the whiskey barrel. Other legislators joined them. The longer the session lasted, the merrier it became. There was dancing on the floor, maudlin singing, an occasional silence to listen to an obscene story, followed by raucous laughter.

Whatever evils had existed in the Old South, such scenes made a mockery of government. And the more these experiences were repeated, the harder the Klan rode, determined to put an end to them.

When the governor of Northern Florida attempted to organize a militia to support his rule, the arms he had procured disappeared as if by magic from the locked and guarded cars of the train that was carrying them from Jacksonville. Less mysterious was the experience of the governor of Arkansas. In Detroit he had purchased several thousand secondhand Belgian muskets and ammunition for them. They were being brought south on the steamboat *Hesper*, but when the *Hesper* reached Memphis, she was boarded by a group of Klansmen who swarmed up her sides from the steam tug *Nellie Jones*. The Klansmen seized the guns and ammunition and hurled both into the muddy Mississippi waters.

Such forays were only part of the Klan program. It was important to deprive the Scalawag-Carpetbagger regimes of the guns that would help to keep them in power, but it was just as important to terrify their new black followers so that they would stay away from the voting booths. And so white-robed night riders descended upon black militia members and black voters, horsewhipping them if they were not frightened by threats. If the whippings did not work, murder sometimes followed.

The most outrageous incident occurred in Union County, South Carolina, where a group of black militia men wantonly killed a one-armed Confederate veteran. Klansmen, wild with fury, raided the jail where the killers were being held, dragged them out, and hanged them from the nearest trees.

By such measures, the Klan in a few brief years began to undermine the structure of government imposed upon the South by the Radicals of the North. Their methods were often rough and even brutal. They were reacting as a totally conquered people who sought by stealth and violence to overthrow their conquerors

The climax came in North Carolina in the election of 1870. It was an election that put the whole scheme of Reconstruction to the test. This was recognized in the North as well as the South. North Carolina's two United States senators got the ear of President Ulysses S.Grant, a great wartime Union general who was a failure in the presidency. The Southerners persuaded Grant to send uniforms and equipment to North Carolina to provide for an armed force that would make certain the balloting came out right.

North Carolina's governor, W. W. Holden, a one-time newspaper publisher, was a well-meaning but indecisive man. He shied at the prospect of open warfare to guarantee the results at the polls, but he was summoned to Washington and had an interview with President Grant. Bucked up by presidential assurances that he had the power of the nation behind him, Holden returned to North Carolina and endorsed military action.

Command of the troops was given to Colonel George W. Kirk, age thirty-three, a daredevil from Tennessee, a swaggering bully noted for his brutality and the many outrages he had committed during the war. It was into the hands of such a man that Governor Holden, proclaiming martial law, entrusted the welfare of his state.

The disaster that followed was predictable. Kirk assembled a small army composed of the lowest kind of poor whites, with a sprinkling of blacks. They were almost all ignorant ragamuffins, human riffraff. Most appeared for service barefooted and in ragged, tattered clothes.

Even after they donned the uniforms that Grant had sent south, they still looked like a bunch of vagabonds.

Six hundred seventy strong, they swaggered out of Morganton, laughing, jeering, and singing obscene songs as they lurched along the highways. They held their guns at haphazard angles and cursed and shouted insults at citizens in the towns through which they passed. On Sundays, they sat around like tramps on a village green, playing cards, cursing, and removing their clothes to offend passing women on their way to church.

All of this was crude horseplay compared to some of their more violent acts. They threatened to burn Salisbury; they bullied the people of Newton at pistol point. As the whim seized them, they made arrests without giving any reason and then tortured their prisoners. Reconstruction judges backed them up; there was no recourse from such lawlessness.

One prisoner was approached by a black soldier, who pointed a pistol at him and shouted, "God damn him, let's hang him—that's the orders we've got." Another prisoner who had no misdeeds to confess was pounced upon by three of these armed vagabonds in the middle of the night. "If you don't confess, I'll break your damned neck tonight," the leader told him.

"Can I put on my shoes?" the helpless man asked.

"No, you will not have any use for them," he was told.

Four pistols were aimed at his breast. "Now will you confess?" he was asked. When the poor man protested he had nothing to tell, a rope was put around his neck, the end thrown over a limb, and he was hoisted aloft until he lost consciousness. When he was lowered and came to, the officer in charge threatened to hang him and leave him, but finally changed his mind and let him go.

On another occasion, Kirk marched his vagabond troops into a Democratic meeting in Yanceyville. He terrorized the gathering, arrested the speakers, and threatened to shoot the women and children.

Such outrages provoked a nationwide storm of protest. Even in North Carolina, despite the presence of Kirk's bushwhackers, angry voices were raised. The result when voters went to the polls was that the Democrats swept the legislature for the first time since Reconstruction began. Governor Holden was impeached. The despicable Kirk fled to Washington, where he found refuge in a job on the capital police force.

The elections of 1870 marked the turning point, for Georgia also rose against the conquerors and the Reconstruction governor was forced to flee. Four other states in the South threw off the occupation yoke in the same year, and General Forrest, deciding that the Klan had served its purpose, ordered his followers to disband and put away their white masks and sheets.

Forrest's action was inspired, not just by the political victories of 1870, but also by the increased difficulty of keeping the Klan under control. Scoundrels of every stripe were hiding behind white sheets and calling themselves Klansmen. It had proved impossible, even though Forrest had been given supreme power, to keep control over every isolated Klavern in the enormous area of the Southern states.

Therefore, the old general, considering his task accomplished, officially disbanded the Klan. The more responsible units obeyed his order, but others continued their night-riding, as well as their intimidating and sometimes murderous ways. They rode for another seven years. Then, after the disputed presidential election of 1876, President Rutherford B. Hayes withdrew federal troops from the South. Reconstruction ended, and with its demise the last remnants of the Klan went out of existence.

CHAPTER 5

THE KLAN IS REBORN

FOR some years after the last federal troops were withdrawn from the South in 1877, the restored white leadership tolerated blacks and, indeed, often relied on their votes. The Klan no longer rode. Violence and lynchings, when they occurred, were the work of lawless rednecks, and poor whites as well as blacks were often the victims.

Then came a new political upheaval, one that ended the brief period of tolerance. The populist movement of 1890 attempted to forge a coalition of poor whites and blacks. It was an alliance that threatened the rule of the conservative white business leadership. Landlords and employers met the threat by herding their black fieldhands and workers to the polls and forcing them to vote "right."

Populist agitators felt they had been cheated; the white leadership felt it had been threatened. From that moment, both forces turned against the blacks. Terror again rode the highways in the form of red-shirted horsemen. In Wilmington, Atlanta, and other Southern cities, mobs assaulted the friendless blacks. The white-black division of Southern society became more acute, with the blacks segregated and once more disenfranchised. Though freed by the Civil War, they were reduced to a station in life little better than slavery.

Such racial hatred was confined largely to the South until 1915. Then a wave of bigotry swept the nation. The Klan was revived in a manner far different from that in the days of Nathan Bedford Forrest. The venom of racial and religious intolerance was injected into the nation's bloodstream. Not just blacks, but Jews, Catholics, and foreign immigrants became objects of the Klan's hatred. White-robed Klansmen began to ride again, proclaiming themselves the only true 100 percent Americans.

This frenzy was sparked by a book and by the classic motion picture that was based on it—*The Birth of a Nation.*

The book was the work of a southern minister, Thomas Dixon, Jr. Dixon had grown up during the Reconstruction era and was imbued with the folk image of the Klan as the savior of the South. A brilliant man, he became a friend of a future President, Woodrow Wilson, while both were graduate students at the Johns Hopkins University. He had a brief fling at politics, then became a Baptist minister. His oratory so moved John D. Rockefeller that Rockefeller talked of building a tabernacle for him. But Dixon was restless. He left the ministry for the lecture platform, and then, finally, he began to write.

His novels created a sensation. The most popular was *The Clansman, an Historic Romance of the Ku Klux Klan,* published in 1905. The book was a melodramatic but vivid portrayal of the worst aspects of Reconstruction. It pictures blacks as wild people. The book's love story is woven around two beautiful southern girls, the image of pure southern womanhood. One, attacked by a black man, flings herself over a cliff and commits suicide to save her virtue. The other, the heroine of the novel, is besieged in an isolated cabin. The Klan rides to save her.

This lurid plot made *The Clansman* a fantastic best-seller, and Dixon, having struck pure gold, turned the novel into a play. He even went on the stage himself, taking a leading role in one of the several road shows that toured the nation. The excitement created by the novel and the play caught the attention of David Wark Griffith, a motion picture pioneer.

Until Griffith came along, movies had been short, slapstick affairs. Griffith decided to turn *The Clansman* into the first full-length picture in movie history. Building upon Dixon's narrative, he traced the history of the nation from the arrival of the first slaves through Civil War battle scenes and on to the horrors of Reconstruction. By the time he had finished, he had completed a two-hour-forty-five-minute epic, which he called *The Birth of a Nation.*

The film played to sell-out crowds paying an unheard-of admission price of two dollars. It was ultimately viewed by some fifty million persons and earned $18 million in profits, an incredible sum in that day. Everywhere the film was shown it played on emotions and raised passions, especially in the South.

The movie's climactic scene was unforgettable. Here is the beautiful heroine surrounded by violent blacks about to break into her cabin. A bugle sounds. The Klansmen mount to ride to the rescue. The orchestra matches thunderous strains from "In the Hall of the Mountain King" to the rhythm of galloping hooves. The camera pans back and forth, switching from shots of the menaced heroine to clips of the onrushing, rescuing Klansmen. Will the heroine be raped? Will the Klansmen get there in time to save her? The tension became almost unbearable as audiences waited for those questions to be answered. In cities of the Old South, men leaped to their feet. They yelled, whooped, and cheered. On one occasion, they became so carried away that they even shot up the screen to save the beautiful heroine from her assailants.

When the picture opened in Atlanta on December 5, 1915, its three-week run coincided with the rebirth of the Klan. Announcements about a new organization for a "high class order of men of intelligence and character" often appeared side by side with newspaper advertisements for the showing of *The Birth of a Nation.*

Some two weeks before the film opened in Atlanta, a strange spectacle had taken place on the granite crest of Stone Mountain, a short distance from the city. Sixteen men had climbed the rocky trail to the summit. There, led by William Joseph Simmons, a fraternal organizer, they had unfurled the American flag in the chilly winds whipping across the crest. Then they had erected a crude cross and set it ablaze while they swore allegiance to the Invisible Empire, Knights of the Ku Klux Klan.

With that scene and with the long-continuing run of *The Birth of a Nation*—brought back time and again for showings in the South—the modern Ku Klux Klan was born.

A Prospective Scene in the "City of Oaks," 4th of March, 1869.

"Hang, curs, hang! * * * * * *Their* complexion is perfect gallows. Stand fast, good
te, to *their* hanging! * * * * * If they be not born to be hanged, our case is miserable."

A Klan warning run in the *Independent Monitor*, Tuscaloosa, Ala., in 1868.

"Dam Your Soul. The Horrible *Sepulchre* and Bloody Moon has at last arrived. Some live to-day to-morrow "*Die.*" We the undersigned understand through our Grand "*Cyclops*" that you have recommended a big Black Nigger for Male agent on our nu rode; wel, sir, Jest you understand in time if he gets on the rode you can make up your mind to pull roape. If you have any thing to say in regard to the Matter, meet the Grand Cyclops and Conclave at Den No. 4 at 12 o'clock midnight, Oct. 1st, 1871.

"When you are in Calera we warn you to hold your tounge and not speak so much with your mouth or otherwise you will be taken on supprise and led out by the Klan and learnt to stretch hemp. Beware. Beware. Beware. Beware.

(Signed)

"PHILLIP ISENBAUM,
"*Grand Cyclops.*
"JOHN BANKSTOWN
"ESAU DAVES.
"MARCUS THOMAS.
"BLOODY BONES.

"You know who. And all others of the Klan."

A facsimile of a Klan warning delivered in Mississippi in 1871

Three Mississippi Klan members after they were arrested in 1872.

A night ride of the Klan in the 1880s.

WIDE WORLD PHOTOS

A scene from the movie *The Birth of a Nation* showing Klansmen riding.

WIDE WORLD PHOTOS

An enrollment meeting of the Klan in Los Angeles in 1925.

CHAPTER

6

A MESSAGE OF HATE

WILLIAM Joseph Simmons, founder of the new Klan, was a large awkward man who had drifted through life with indifferent success until he found a gold mine in purveying hate.

Born in central Alabama in 1880, he had been reared on stories of the old Klan and the manner in which it had saved the South. Though he adopted the title of "colonel," he had fought in the Spanish-American War without ever rising above the rank of private.

His father had been a physician, but Simmons was too poor to get a medical education. Back from the war, he experienced, he later claimed, a religious conversion and turned to preaching. It was a vocation that developed his oratorical talents.

For twelve years, he rode the backwoods circuit, preaching in poor churches in Alabama and Florida, always hoping for the day when the Methodist Church, South, would asssign him to a big church worthy of his talents. The leaders of the church, however, apparently sensed the buncombe in the man, for in 1912 they dismissed him for inefficiency and moral impairment.

Defrocked, Simmons became a salesman. This led him eventually into the financially rewarding field of fraternal organizing and fund-raising. He joined several varieties of Masons, was a member of the Knights Templar, and was so successful in organizing Woodmen of the World that he commanded five "regiments" and was called "colonel." Such lodge work gave the former down-at-heel minister an income of some $15,000 a year, veritable wealth at that time. It also pointed the way to a more glorious future.

Simmons always contended that it wasn't *The Birth of a Nation* that gave him the idea for a Klan revival. He had been dreaming about reestablishing the Klan for twenty years, he always said, and he told a fantastic story about the vision that had inspired him.

The official history, *Knights of the Ku Klux Klan,* gives this version as related by Simmons: "He was then a poor minister in Alabama, and one summer night...he thought he caught sight of something mysterious and strange in the sky, and as he looked at the clouds, a row of horses seemed to be galloping across the horizon. White-robed figures were on the steeds. The clouds seemed to disperse, and a rough outline of the United States appeared in the background. The horses remained, and then one big problem after another of American life moved across the map.

"He fell to his knees and offered a prayer to God, so he said, to help solve the mystery of the apparitions he had seen in the sky. He then registered a vow that a great patriotic fraternal order should be builded as a memorial to the heroes of our nation. That was the real beginning of the Knights of the Ku Klux Klan."

Even Simmons never claimed that the ghostly riders had sounded the bugle for the charge, but he had heard the call for action anyway. Later, when he was injured in an automobile accident and was laid up for three months, he spent his time drafting plans and perfecting the organization of his future order. His concept was dictatorial. He was to be the Imperial Wizard of the Invisible Empire. All power would flow downward from him. He alone could appoint and remove national officers, issue and revoke chapter charters. He divided the Invisible Empire into eight districts, each consisting of a group of states. Each would be headed by a Grand Dragon. Grand Titans would head provinces, each a congressional district, and Exalted Cyclopes (referred to as E.C.'s) would command the local Klaverns, the lowest groups in the Klan. Fund-raisers were to be known as Kleagles.

Simmons mapped out the whole scheme in a 54-page pamphlet he called the *Kloran*. He included in it even the secret jargon to be used for initiating members into the Klan. This mumbo jumbo was supposed to be known only to Klan members, but Simmons, with a canny foresight for his own financial future, ripped aside the veil of secrecy. He had the *Kloran* copyrighted on January 16, 1917. Because copyright laws require that two copies of a manuscript must be filed with the Library of Congress in Washington, anyone who was interested could read all about the innermost "secrets" of the Klan.

When a new recruit was to be admitted into the Klan, he was annointed with oil from a vessel on the "sacred altar" with these words: "With this transparent, lifegiving, powerful God-given fluid, more precious and far more significant than all the sacred oils of the ancients, I set you apart from the men of your daily association to the great and honorable task you have voluntarily allotted yourselves as citizens of the Invisible Empire..."

With this structure perfected, on paper at least, Simmons was ready to spring into action when *The Birth of a Nation* took the South by storm. Within a few weeks after he took his initial band up the rocky slopes of Stone Mountain, Simmons had gathered ninety recruits for the new Klan. Each new member paid him a ten-dollar initiation fee. And to each he sold the white garb of the order and life insurance. This was just the first sampling of the financial waters.

When the United States entered World War I, Simmons saw and seized his first great patriotic opportunity. Slackers, idlers, strike leaders, immoral women must be dealt with. When shipyards in Mobile, Alabama, were threatened with a strike in the summer of 1918, a flying squadron of Simmons's white-sheeted Klansmen descended upon the yards, seized a labor leader, and threatened all "idlers and draft dodgers." The pattern was repeated in Birmingham, where a strike leader mysteriously disappeared just as a walkout was about to be called at some of the mills near the city. In Montgomery, the Klan warned loose women to keep away from the soldiers at Camp Sheridan. No one interviewed the soldiers to see whether they appreciated the Klan's action.

Patriotic parades were held everywhere in those days of wartime fervor; and in the South, wherever there was a parade, there were the sheet-covered Klansmen holding aloft the flag. Such activities enabled Simmons to increase his membership to several thousand by 1920. The dues and purchases of raiment were his reward for patriotism. Still, despite this growth, the Klan remained a small regional organization, confined to the states of Alabama and Georgia. Its potential for wealth and mischief had not begun to be tapped.

Simmons, with his visions of ghostly horsemen riding in the sky, was a dreamer. He lacked long-range vision and executive ability. To become a truly formidable national force, the Klan needed high-powered public relations—a propaganda blitz that was now to be supplied by a couple of experts.

They were Edward Young Clark, a one-time journalist, and Mrs. Elizabeth Tyler, a divorced woman. Clarke was in his thirties, slim and graceful, with curly dark hair. He had about him a nervous intensity that passed for drive. Mrs. Tyler, a large woman, had blue eyes and auburn hair. She dressed in black and spoke in a decisive manner. She impressed audiences with her forcefulnes.

Clark and Mrs.Tyler had formed the Southern Publicity Association. They had handled drives for the Red Cross, the Salvation Army, and the Anti-Saloon League. They were together in Atlanta, he running a

Harvest Home festival and she, a Better Babies Parade. And there they and Simmons met.

Simmons needed a boost for his Klan, and the Clarke-Tyler team saw the possibility of cashing in. They offered to run a national publicity campaign for Simmons, but they did not come cheap. They told him they wanted 80 percent of every ten-dollar membership fee they collected, and they wanted two dollars out of the membership fees that Klan chapters might collect on their own. Simmons agreed, and in June, 1920, a contract was signed giving Clarke full charge of recruitment.

The two promoters soon changed the fundamental nature of the Klan. Fraternity, secrecy, white supremacy, and patriotism were all fine, but the Klan, they thought, needed something more—something that would really steam up the public on a nationwide scale.

The times were ripe for promoters of hysteria. World War I—the war that had been fought "to save the world for democracy"—had ended in a flawed peace that made the world less safe than ever. All the killing and sacrifice, it seemed, had been for nothing. Europe was in turmoil, more sharply divided than ever. The communists had seized power in Russia. Foreign immigrants were flooding into the United States. There was a brief depression. All forces combined to make Americans ripe for the Klan's call for a return to "100 percent Americanism."

The Clarke-Tyler team decided to play on all these hidden fears and frustrations. No longer was it enough to see that the black was "put in his place and kept there." Now there was a whole host of enemies to be fought, hidden foes who might have Americans all across the continent quaking in their beds. The Klan was quick to identify this menace. It was the work of foreigners, radicals, Catholics, Jews—and, of course, blacks. The Klan alone stood for "100 percent Americanism," and the only 100 percent pure Americans who could join its ranks were white Protestants.

"Colonel" Simmons emphasized the Klan's new pitch in dramatic fashion. A tall man, he had thin, firm lips; a long, thin, prominent nose; and thinning red hair. Towering above an audience of Georgia Klansmen, he said not a word as he drew a Colt automatic from one pocket and plunked it down on the table before him. Still silent, he took a revolver from another pocket and thumped that down on the table, too. Then, in one final, dramatic gesture, he whipped out a bowie knife and plunged it, the blade quivering, into the middle of his arsenal on the table.

"Now," he thundered, "let the niggers, Catholics, Jews, and all others who disdain my imperial wizardy come on."

The campaign of racial and religious hatred had begun.

CHAPTER 7

VIOLENCE FOR A PRICE

WITH the Clarke-Tyler team rounding up new recruits for the Klan at ten dollars a head, the character of Simmons's original organization changed radically. Some of the leading citizens of Atlanta had been among Simmons's first followers, but once the object became the gathering of as many ten-dollar memberships as possible, fewer questions were asked about the character of the new recruits. Any roughneck willing to put up his ten dollars could hide under the white sheets of the order.

Financially, the recruiting drive was a bonanza. Clark sent his hustlers across the country, and in the first fifteen months of his operation, he added 85,000 members to the rolls of the Klan. At ten dollars a head, this meant $850,000 in revenue. And this was only the beginning. There were other sources to tap.

The Gate City Manufacturing Company was set up in Atlanta as the sole manufacturer of Klan regalia. The Searchlight Publishing Company controlled the growing volume of Klan printing and publications.

A realty company owned by Clarke managed the Klan's real estate holdings, with a large part of the profits going into Clarke's own pocket.

Simmons fared well also. His share of the membership take came to some $170,000. In addition, the Klan rewarded him with $25,000 in back pay for his devotion during the lean years and gave him a $33,000 suburban home, which he named Klan Krest.

As can be seen, the rogues at the top of the new Klan movement were doing very well for themselves. They achieved such success by welding together the highest and the lowest motives. They preached loudly the principles of old-time religion—and, in the name of holiness, they countenanced and encouraged whiplashings, lynchings, and murders.

Their lofty pitch was made to fundamentalist Protestant pastors and their congregations. The Klan, coming into a new town, always tried to get the Protestant ministers on its side. A pastor would be urged to accept free membership in the Klan and to become an officer of the local Klavern. Hundreds did. Some even abandoned their flocks to become full-time organizers for the Klan. Often, when the Klan found a sympathetic minister, its members would appear in the middle of a Sunday service. Clad in their white robes, they would march solemnly down the aisles, massing in front of the pulpit while they presented the church with a donation of thirty-five or fifty dollars.

Klan lectures paid lip service to all the ideals of "100 percent Americanism"—motherhood, chastity, temperance, "clean motion pictures, and decent literature." One popular broadside summed up the Klan's professed principles in these words:

"Every criminal, every gambler, every thug, every libertine, every girl ruiner, every home wrecker, every wifebeater, every dope peddler, every moonshiner, every crooked politican, every pagan Papist priest, every shyster lawyer, every K. of C. [Knights of Columbus], every white slaver, every brothel madam, every Rome controlled newspaper, every black spider—is fighting the Klan. Think it over. Which side are you on?"

The message made it obvious that the enemies of the Klan were everywhere in American society. And it followed that the Klan would seek out and punish them, setting itself up as judge, jury, and executioner. The Klan, in other words, was inherently a vigilante organization. It could commit the most atrocious acts under the guise of high principle. And the perpetrators of those acts would be hidden behind white masks and protected by Klan secrecy.

This propensity for uncontrolled violence quickly made itself felt in the South, where the Klan originally was strongest. Texas and Louisiana were two states in which the Klan soon acquired powerful political influence—a power that protected it even when it committed the worst crimes. In Texas, Klan Klaverns in Houston, Dallas, and lesser municipalities ran amok.

A black dentist in Houston was kidnapped and whipped, apparently for no offense except that his skin was black. A white man in Timpson was taken out and beaten because he had recently separated from his wife. A man who spoke German, a divorced man in Dallas, an attorney who handled lawsuits for blacks and, what was worse, sometimes won—all were lashed.

A woman was taken from a hotel where she worked, stripped, beaten with a wet rope, then tarred and feathered. Her offense? There was some question whether she had been properly divorced before her second marriage. Waco police arrested three hooded Klansmen, but a grand jury refused to indict them.

The Klan in Dallas went on a flogging spree. During the spring of 1922, it wielded the lash on sixty-eight persons, most of them in a special Klan whipping-meadow along the Trinity River bottom. Some accounts charged the Texas Klan with more than 500 whipping and tar-and-feathering parties. In addition, there were all kinds of other threats, assaults, and even homicides.

Bad as it was, the Texas experience was relatively mild compared to what happened in Louisiana. There the Klan raged so out of control that it virtually superseded the government. Governor John M. Parker was forced to appeal to the U. S. Justice Department for help because courts and police were in the hands of the Klan and he felt certain that his own mail and telephones were being tampered with.

The worst atrocity occurred in Morehouse Parish near the Arkansas border. There the postmaster, judge, sheriff, prosecuting attorney, and police officers were all Klan members. There had been new oil and gas discoveries around the town of Bastrop, and roughnecks flooded into the area to work the new fields. They were a rootless, tough gang of men. With little to do after work, they joined the Klan and found their entertainment in riding the countryside at night and flogging anyone who happened to cross their path.

The Klan in the region was headed by Captain J. K. Skipworth, who had been mayor of Bastrop before the war. Old Skip, as he was called, enjoyed giving orders and was puffed up with his own importance. But, according to Justice Department investigators later, he was more of a figurehead than an actual commander. Real authority in the Klan was vested in Dr. B. M. McKoin, who lived in the neighboring town of Mer Rouge. Dr. McKoin was unhappy because his own town was not as avid about the Klan as were the residents of Bastrop. And so he decided to stir things up.

Going out one night apparently to answer a sick call, he took his Ford car into the woods and pumped some bullets into the back of it. Then he returned to town and charged that a criminal gang had tried to kill him.

The Klansmen in the area immediately jumped to a conclusion about the identity of the men who were supposed to have committed this act. Their suspects—and to be suspected by the Klan was as good as being convicted—were Watt Daniels, a planter's son, and his close friend, Tom Richards, a garage mechanic.

Daniels and Richards were known to have been bad-mouthing the Klan. They had actually been caught spying at one Klan meeting. And so, when Dr. McKoin concocted his phony story about an assassination attempt, the Klansmen seized Daniels and Richards. They dragged their captives into the woods, accused them of having tried to shoot the doctor, then eventually turned them loose, with a warning to watch their conduct and keep their mouths shut.

The two young men apparently weren't the kind to be intimidated. They didn't heed the warning, but kept right on criticizing the Klan. The Klan decided the time had come to teach Daniels, Richards, and any other like-minded critics a lesson no one would ever forget.

A barbecue and baseball game were held in Bastrop on August 24, 1922. A large crowd of spectators from both Bastrop and Mer Rouge attended. After the game, cars driving back to Mer Rouge found the road blocked. An automobile had been stopped right across the highway.

As soon as the cars coming from the baseball game stopped, they were surrounded by swarming Klansmen, masked and carrying shot guns. The Klansmen had cut off all roads between Bastrop and Mer Rouge. They had commandeered the ferry. They had cut the telephone lines. They had made certain no one could escape their net; no one could send out a cry for help.

A white-robed spotter went down the line of cars blocked on the road. When he came to the car carrying Watt Daniels, he stopped, pointed, and said: "That's the man we want."

Women screamed as Daniels, Richards, their fathers, and another man were dragged out of the cars. The captives were blindfolded, hog-tied, and heaved into the back of a Ford truck.

The truck roared away in a cloud of dust. When it reached an isolated spot, it halted, and the captives were dragged to a clearing in the woods. Daniel's father, who was seventy, and one of the other prisoners were tied to trees and lashed with leather straps. Watt

Daniels managed to loosen his bonds and charged at the Klansmen, trying to reach his father. In the struggle that followed, young Daniels ripped the mask away from the face of one of the Klansmen. He recognized the wearer and called out a name. Daniels was quickly over-powered, but the damage had been done. His friend, Richards, had either heard the name he called or recognized the face behind the ripped edges of the mask. In either event, Daniels and Richards now knew too much for their own good.

The Klansmen dragged them deeper into the forest. Later that night, they released the three older men. But young Daniels and Richards disappeared as if the earth had swallowed them.

Residents of the two towns now armed themselves as if for civil war. Old Skip, fearing an attack from his enraged neighbors in Mer Rouge, deployed a shotgun brigade around the courthouse in Bastrop, checked the mails and telephones, and examined all who passed through town to see if they were carrying arms.

This was the situation when Governor Parker appealed to Washington for help. His letter said in part:

"Due to the activities of an organized body reputed to be the Ku Klux Klan...not only have the laws been violated, but men taken out, beaten and whipped. Two men have been brutally murdered without trial or charges...My information is that six more citizens have been ordered to leave their homes (in Morehouse Parish) under penalty of death. These conditions are beyond the control of the Governor of this State...A number of law officers and others charged with the enforcement of law in this State are publicly recognized as members of this Ku Klux Klan."

Though the U.S. Justice Department had no authority to investigate murder—a crime that would have to be tried in state courts—it decided to send in agents to help Governor Parker restore order. Klansmen in Bastrop boasted that they knew who the agents were and that they would "take care of them" as they had taken care of Daniels and Richards. But the Justice Department agents were not stupid. While one group made its activities fairly obvious, a second undercover squad worked quietly and secretly, unknown to the Klan.

These sleuths gathered enough information to be certain in a general way about what had happened. They knew that Daniels and Richards had been killed and that their bodies had been weighted and sunk in one of the deep lakes of the parish.

With great courage, considering the prevailing mood in Louisiana, Governor Parker now publicly denounced the Klan. He lashed out at it in speeches at the governors' conference in Hot Springs, Virginia, in Chicago, and in several cities in his own state. The Klan greeted such attacks with contempt. A pro-Klan minister wrote in a local paper: "Lyncher John and Dago Cocacola [the governor and attorney general] have been transformed by the witchcraft of Romanism." Then the Klan held a big rally near Baton Rouge and initiated one thousand new members.

Governor Parker responded by sending a company of infantry into the Bastrop area to protect workers dragging the lakes in the hunt for the bodies of Daniels and Richards. While this work was going on, a heavy charge of dynamite went off one night in Lake Lafourche. The explosion brought two badly mangled bodies to the surfce. Daniels and Richards had been found.

Authorities never discovered who had set off the dynamite charge. The generally accepted theory was that Klansmen themselves had done it, hoping to destroy the bodies and the evidence of murder. Instead, the blast had dislodged the corpses and brought them to the surface.

The state government threw a cordon of infantrymen and machine gunners around the courthouse in Bastrop while a grand jury was assembled to consider the evidence. Several witnesses, subpoenaed before the grand jury, identified the Klansmen who had abducted the two murdered men. The Klan, amazingly, contended that Daniels and

Richards were still alive. It produced scrawled notes, allegedly signed by the two men, that had been mailed from various parts of the nation. Two grand juries heard the evidence. Both contained a large number of Klansmen. Both refused to indict anyone, but merely reported that the parish needed a new jail and repairs to the courthouse roof.

Justice had been completely defied by the new "100 percent Americans." But Governor Parker did not give up. He held open hearings on Klan night-riding. He pressed for conviction of Klan members on lesser charges. Old Skip was fined ten dollars for raiding a still.

More effective than the law was the public fire that Governor Parker trained on the Klan. He publicized the names of Klan members. He refused to promote several district judges because they belonged to the Klan. He appointed a Jewish sheriff in Morehouse Parish. These measures had an effect. Public opinion began to change, and Klan candidates who had been riding high, began to lose elections. Some of the Klansmen who had been identified as among the sheeted goons who had killed Daniels and Richards fled the state.

Something had been accomplished, but no one could contend that justice had been done. The ruthless persons who had killed Daniels and Richards had not been tried and punished. Klan influence and the prejudice it created had been too powerful for that. It was a pattern that was to be repeated time and again forty years later during the civil rights movement of the 1960s.

THE BACKFIRE

CHAPTER 8

THE outrages being committed by the Klan under the cloak of 100 percent Americanism turned the stomachs of many Americans and soon drew a critical barrage from the nation's press. Many of the more responsible citizens who had joined "Colonel" Simmons's movement dropped out, but they were more than replaced by Clarke's ten-dollars-a-head recruits.

For a time, it seemed that every setback was a boost. Whatever the Klan lost on one hand, it more than gained on the other. Typical was the reaction across the nation when the New York *World*, one of the great newspapers of its day, loosed a twenty-one-day barrage at the Klan, beginning September 6, 1921.

Herbert Bayard Swope, one of the foremost editors of the time, was the first to see that the Klan was a national menace and to concentrate on exposing it. One day in 1920, a small, crudely wrapped package, addressed to Swope, was delivered at the newspaper's office. Attached to it was a note saying that the *World's* plant would "be blowed up by we all, Ku Klux, tomorrow, at noon."

The morrow came and "we all" didn't do any blowing up. The package addressed to Swope contained some harmless junk—rubber tubing, wires, and a broken cigar. It never could be determined whether the package was the work of a prankster or whether it had been intended by the Klan as a threat. In any event, it was enough to set Swope's editorial juices flowing. On Sunday, October 20, 1920, the *World's* weekend feature section carried a front-page story. It was datelined Atlanta and began, "The old Ku Klux Klan of Reconstruction days has been revived. Hooded night riders in long, flowing white gowns parade the thoroughfares and bypaths of the South in the dark hours when innocent people are abed."

It was just a sample of what was to come. The *World's* attack on the Klan was greatly aided by that old bumbler, "Colonel" Simmons himself. Simmons had conducted a long correspondence with "a friend" in the North whom he believed to be a transplanted Anglo-Saxon Southerner. Actually, Simmons's "friend" was Walter White, of the National Association for the Advancement of Colored People, one of the most militant Negro leaders in the nation. To White, Simmons indiscreetly boasted about the "achievements" of his new Klan—and White passed the information along to Herbert Bayard Swope.

A second windfall fell into Swope's lap. Henry P. Fry, a retired army captain from Chattanooga, had joined the Klan early in 1921, thinking it was just a fraternal order. When he discovered what it was actually like, Fry became disenchanted and turned detective. He managed to get hold of membership lists, copies of application questionnaires, the texts of secret oaths, and other information. In June, he brought his files to Swope, who promptly bought the information.

Rowland Thomas, one of the *World's* best reporters and rewrite men, whipped the material into shape, and for three weeks Swope gave the day-by-day exposé the leading page-one headline in his newspaper. In New York, where the *World* had many Catholic, Jewish, and black readers, the series was a sensation. The newspaper's circulation jumped by 60,000. But elsewhere across the nation the reaction was lukewarm; indeed, in many places, it was positively hostile.

Rural America has an anti–big city bias, especially where New York City is concerned. It is an enduring bias, one on which President Richard M. Nixon and Vice-President Spiro Agnew were to play years later in the congressional elections of 1970 and the presidential campaign of 1972. In the 1920s, this animosity was even more deep-seated than Nixon and Agnew found it a half-century later, and the *World's* attack on the Klan backfired outside the cities.

New members flocked to join the Klan by the thousands. According to Simmons, many came in with coupons that they had clipped from the *World* and other papers running the series. "It wasn't until the newspapers began to attack the Klan that it really grew," Simmons recalled years later.

This initial reaction was the very opposite of what Swope and the *World* had desired, but the *World*, which was later to receive a Pulitzer prize for its Klan exposé, had the last word. It had sunk so many harpoons into the great white carcass of the Klan that the barbs penetrated deep and festered.

One disclosure that was especially embarrassing to an organization devoted to the protection of pure white womanhood dealt with the liaison between Clarke and Mrs. Tyler. The *World* had discovered that, in 1919, the pair had been arrested, less than fully clad and less than sober, during a police raid on a house of ill repute. They had been fined five dollars apiece for disorderly conduct. In what seemed like an attempted cover-up, the page of the police docket that contained the account of their indiscretion had been removed.

Clarke had a weak excuse. He claimed that he had done nothing wrong, that the raid had been instigated by his estranged wife. It was an explanation that did not serve in an organization like the Klan that whiplashed men and women for misbehavior and for wrecking the foundation of the home. Some of the Klan's field representatives were so enraged at what Clarke and Mrs. Tyler had done to the Klan's moral image that they demanded the pair be dismissed. Instead, Simmons fired the protesting field representatives. It was only the first of many serious schisms in the Invisible Empire.

The *World's* devastating account of Klan brutalities had been too specific to be ignored. The *World* had made it clear that the Klan had violated a whole series of Amendments to the Constitution, especially the First, Fourth, Fifth, Sixth and Thirteenth. The First Amendment, of course, guarantees the right to freedom of religion and freedom of speech; the Fourth protects the people "against unreasonable searches and seizures," as in the case of Daniels and Richards; the Fifth and Sixth guarantee that no one shall be held without an indictment by a grand jury or punished without a fair trial. The Thirteenth Amendment, passed during the Civil War, abolished slavery and "involuntary servitude." The Klan's actions made clear that it had defied and violated every one of these basic guarantees of American freedom and justice.

Nevertheless, President Warren G. Harding and the Justice Department refused to act. The problem, they said, was one to be handled by the states. The Rules Committee of the U.S. House of Representatives was more concerned, however, and scheduled public hearings on the Klan for October, 1921.

Clarke went into a funk. His friend, Mrs. Tyler, became disgusted with his weak-kneed attitude and had to prop him up to see the issue through. The Klan tried to pretend that *it* was the victim of persecution, and to support its contention, it had a fake attempt made on the life of Mrs. Tyler. All of this mattered little. The real struggle came when congressmen questioned "Colonel" Simmons.

The "Colonel" was at his best, or the congressmen were at their worst; it was hard to determine which. In any event, Simmons led his inquisitors in a merry dance around the Maypole. He had intended, he said, only to found a fraternal order—a lodge like many others in the country. He knew nothing about brutality and violence. If these deeds had been committed, it was by a few wrongdoers (every organization has its share, doesn't it?), and the Klan as a whole should not be held responsible.

Simmons had appeared, protesting that he was in poor health, and in his third and final day on the witness stand, he gave a dramatic performance. He rocked back and forth unsteadily on his feet as he described how he had suffered from treasonable actions within the Klan. Caesar had his Brutus, Washington his Arnold, he proclaimed. Then: "If this organization is unworthy, let me know it and I will destroy it, but if it is not, then let it stand." He turned to the spectators in one final gesture, his voice rising as he called on "the Father to forgive those who have persecuted the Klan."

Then he swayed and collapsed senseless on the floor.

It was tremendous theater, and the Klan emerged from the congressional inquiry virtually unscathed. But, as Simmons was to find, there was a heavy price to pay.

The scandal concerning Clarke and Mrs. Tyler would not go away, and it was disrupting the Klan. Four of the organization's leading northern sales representatives met in Washington and decided that Clarke and Mrs. Tyler would have to be ousted. They went to Atlanta and talked to Simmons. He told them he knew that they were right; he promised to act—then did nothing.

The unhappy dissidents went to the newspapers. They accused Clarke of padding payrolls, misappropriating funds and holding a Svengali-like sway over the ailing Simmons. Clarke sued; they countersued. This was the beginning of a whole series of lawsuits that benefited only the lawyers and washed the Klan's dirty linen in public. Thus the foundation was laid for a palace coup at the summit of the Invisible Empire.

The master conniver was a one-time cut-rate dentist from Dallas,

Hiram Wesley Evans. He was a roly-poly glad-hander, a compulsive joiner and lodge man. He also had a fine hand for intrigue.

He had been valuable to Mrs. Tyler in combating an anti-Klan movement among the Masons in Texas, and she had brought Evans to Atlanta headquarters. There one of Simmons's chief aides, L. D. Wade, fell from grace after being found by police in what was called "an embarrassing circumstance." Such embarrassing circumstances always seemed to be catching up with leaders of the Klan, and there was worse to come. At the moment, however, Wade's misfortune was Hiram Evans's good luck. He replaced Wade in charge of the party secretariat, and he used this pivotal position to scheme for the overthrow of Simmons.

He had help. Younger Klan leaders had become convinced that Simmons was too weak; Clarke, too greedy. Scandals were hurting the Klan, and the only solution was to change the leadership.

Six conspirators met in the Piedmont Hotel in Atlanta to plot the overthrow of the Imperial Wizard. The two most important figures were Evans, who intended to become the Wizard himself, and David C. Stephenson, the fantastically successful Indiana Klan leader who had his eyes on two things: women and the White House.

Stephenson was eager to avoid a floor fight at the forthcoming first annual Klonvokation of the Klan. He favored giving Simmons $1,000 a month and kicking him upstairs with the meaningless title of Emperor of the Klan while the real power would be vested in Evans as the new Imperial Wizard. There was just one problem: how to get Simmons to agree to his own removal from power without realizing what he was doing?

The plotters decided that Stephenson and Fred Savage, chief investigator for the Klan, should visit the Imperial Wizard and try to pull the wool over his eyes. They called on him at three o'clock in the morning at his home at 1840 Peachtree Street. Simmons had been out drinking, had just returned home, and was probably not too alert as a consequence. Certainly, he was no match for Savage and Stephenson.

They convinced him that, if he let his name go before the convention for reelection as Imperial Wizard, there were some rowdies ready to attack him and there might be a bloody battle on the floor. This would stroy the Klan. Why not avoid it by beating his enemies to the draw? parate the offices and duties at the top; have himself named Emperor for life and Evans made Imperial Wizard. Simmons, despite his recent alcoholic intake, got a whiff of something he didn't like. He objected to Evans. But, he was told, Evans's elevation would be only temporary; he would serve only until things in the ranks quieted down. On this basis, Simmons agreed to cut his own throat.

Not until the deed had been done, not until it was too late, did he realize that he had been stripped of all power, that Hiram Evans was not just a temporary Imperial Wizard but a permanent one. Simmons's downfall was soon followed by that of Edward Young Clarke. The fund-raiser, who still handled the golden stream flowing into the Atlanta headquarters, had lost his helpmate. Mrs. Tyler quit Klan affairs to get married. To assuage his loneliness, Clarke paid the fare for a pretty Houston girl, the sister of a bank robber, to come to New Orleans to meet him. This was a violation of the federal Mann Act forbidding the transportation of women across state lines for immoral purposes. Clarke was indicted, convicted, fined. Again his name was in the headlines in a manner that did not square with the Klan's claim to be the protector of pure womanhood and the custodian of morality. Clarke was quickly stripped of all his powers, his contract canceled.

Simmons and Clarke later sued the Klan; the Klan sued them right back. The litigation would last for two more years, but Simmons and Clarke were finished with the Klan.

The big winners in the Atlanta palace coup were Hiram Evans and D. C. Stephenson. Evans reigned unchallenged as the Klan's Imperial Wizard, and Stephenson was confirmed as head of the Indiana Klan, and made Grand Dragon of twenty-two states.

CHAPTER 9

THE KLAN SPREADS

ONE of the most amazing things about the Klan movement of the 1920s was the way it engulfed the entire nation. Its early popularity in the South was understandable. There, for centuries, racial distrust, fear, and hatred had run like an ugly stream under the surface of southern life. The black man was a readily identifiable target, and once passions were aroused, it was easy to channel hate and violence against any persons or groups that dared to oppose the Klan.

Clarke and Mrs. Tyler, of course, had broadened the basis of prejudice. They had added the Catholic and the Jew to the Negro on the Klan's hate list. They had publicized the Klan as the champion of Americanism on a broad range of public issues, ranging from private morality to the breakdown of law and order. This gave the Klan a wide range of "enemies" to fight, but the mere identification of the new, innumerable foes does not explain the frenzy that swept the nation from the northeastern states through the Midwest and on out to the far Pacific coast in California and Oregon.

As a boy, I saw it happen, and I remember the emotional idiocies it spawned. My parents' home was in Point Pleasant, New Jersey, and this area along the Ocean-Monmouth County coastline in central New Jersey was a hotbed of Klan activity. One of our neighbors, a man who had been the bustling manager of one of the larger local food stores, suddenly quit his job and for several years occupied himself mowing his lawn by day in summer and attending Klan rallies by night. He was, we heard, a Kleagle in the Invisible Empire, and the visible evidence seemed to say that the empire supported him well.

Everywhere one turned in those days, one found neighbors, who until then had seemed rational, caught up in the Klan frenzy and giving credence to the wildest fantasies. They reacted especially to the Catholic "menace." They actually believed that the Pope had plans to seize control of the nation's government. When New York Governor Alfred E. Smith, a Catholic, became the leading candidate for the Democratic presidential nomination in 1924, reason took a permanent vacation.

No tale was too fantastic to be believed. The most preposterous story went like this: If Al Smith was elected President, the Pope would have a secret tunnel dug to the basement of the White House so that he could zip in and out and tell the President what to do. How the Pope in the Vatican in Rome was to accomplish this miracle of modern engineering wasn't even considered. Mature and supposedly sensible persons discussed this fantasy with the utmost seriousness as if, indeed, it was a real possibility, an imminent threat.

Rural areas like ours in New Jersey were, of course, ideal breeding grounds for bigotry. As it was predominantly white at that time (there were only two or three black families in our whole town), race was not an issue, but religion was. A strong fundamentalist strain ran through large Methodist and Baptist congregations in the region. In some churches, card-playing was regarded as a sin; dancing was frowned on; even the movies, just becoming popular, were looked upon with suspicion. For such rigid, old-time Protestants, the Catholic church was the instrument of the Devil, and the Pope was believed, actually, to have concealed horns.

Such religious fanaticism and prejudice in rural areas like ours might explain the spread of the Klan there and the hold it had on its followers. But the Klan's amazing strength was not confined to such isolated rural pockets. It flourished everywhere—in the cities of the East, the cities of the Midwest, and the open reaches of Oregon, one of the most intellectually alive and progressive states in the nation. How does one explain this phenomenon? How does one account for the wildfire spread of a movement that appealed to the basest elements of human nature?

The answer seems contained in one word: *threat.* The Klan burst on the American scene just at a time when American life seemed to many to be threatened on every side. The threats, real or imagined, were different for different regions, but a threat was all the Klan needed to get a foothold. Its Kleagles were instructed to find out what most worried and concerned citizens in areas the movement was trying to organize—and then to concentrate on that particular threat, making the Klan the one and only protector of the people.

A postwar depression had put thousands out of work, especially in the cities. At the same time, a new wave of immigrants flooded our shores. These newly arrived foreigners seemed to native Americans more foreign than those who had come before. They were not, for the most part, Northern Europeans but Slavs, Italians, and Jews from Poland and Russia. The native-born worker, thrown out of his job by the depression, saw himself doubly threatened by the competition these newcomers posed in a tight labor market. And so it was easy to sow in his mind the seeds of anti-Catholic, anti-Semitic, and anti-foreign prejudice.

In many cities of the industrial Midwest, the threat was essentially the same, but with a different cast. During World War I (just as was to happen later during World War II), blacks and poor whites had begun to move from the fields of the South, where they had scrabbled for a living, to seek employment in the war-humming factories of the Midwest industrial heartland. Foreigners, too, came to compete for jobs in steel factories and mills, and when jobs became scarce in the postwar slump, the Klan found the climate fertile for its emotional appeals.

None of this quite explains how the Klan, for one brief period, nearly took control of the state of Oregon. Seemingly, it would be hard to find a less likely ground for spreading the Klan virus of hate and suspicion. Illiteracy was almost unknown in Oregon. The population was white and 85 percent native-born. There were few blacks in the state; there were few Catholics. Yet the Klan invaded and acquired such power in Oregon that the governor, like Governor Parker in Louisiana, appealed to the federal government for help.

When the Klan swept into Oregon in 1921, it used its tried and tested technique. It looked for a local issue that had people concerned. It found it in lax law enforcement. In Oregon, as in most other states, the Prohibition amendment was being openly flouted. Bootleggers and speakeasy proprietors catered to the business of those who wanted their liquor and did not care how they got it. Law enforcement, swiftly corrupted, winked at blatant violations of the law. This issue gave the Klan its needed opening wedge.

Within a week, the Klan had signed up one hundred members in Jackson County. It started a movement to recall the sheriff. It gained the support of the Women's Christian Temperance Union and several churches. Backed by such respectable groups, it began to carry on in its usual fashion. It seized a convicted black bootlegger, put a rope around his neck, and hoisted him in the air until his toes barely touched the ground. Nearly strangled, the bootlegger was released with a warning to get out of town—and he did. A white salesman who was suing a Klansman got similar treatment. The Klan had begun to purge wrongdoers and its own foes with a vengeance.

Next came the vicious spreading of religious hate. Though Catholics were only a tiny minority in Oregon, evangelists and Klan sympathizers magnified them into a menace. Crosses were burned on hillsides. Supposedly "escaped nuns" were brought in to tell audiences horrifying stories about their treatment. Klan demagogues denounced "the Roman octopus which has taken over control of the nation's capital." They appealed to the white Protestant population, declaring, "This is a white, Protestant, and Gentile man's country, and they are going to run it."

The Klan stopped at nothing to make its presence known and felt. An American flag was nailed to the steeple of a Roman Catholic church. An editor who tried to expose the Klan for false anti-Catholic tirades was boycotted. The press in most of Oregon may have taken a cue from his example, for studies later showed that some 80 percent of the state's newspapers never mentioned the Klan at a time when the Klan was virtually capturing the state.

The hooded order elected officials in a number of cities. Candidates for state office came hat in hand to its headquarters in Portland, begging for its help. Klan power was so strong that authorities in Medford refused to investigate three atrocities that the Klan labeled mere "practice lynchings." Appalled, Governor Ben Olcott appealed to Washington for help, but he was told that the federal government could not send agents into Oregon because no federal laws had been violated.

In 1922, Governor Olcott told the governors' conference, "We woke up one morning and found the Klan had about gained political control of the state. Practically, not a word had been raised against them."

Such outspokenness made Governor Olcott a Klan target. When he ran for reelection in 1922, the Klan supported his Democratic opponent, and Olcott was soundly defeated in normally Republican Oregon. In 1923, Klan-backed candidates for the state legislature were elected everywhere, and the Klan picked the president of the state senate and the speaker of the house. This was the high-water mark of Klan influence in Oregon.

In one short year, its movement collapsed. The struggle for power in Atlanta that resulted in the ouster of Simmons splintered the Oregon Klan into opposing factions. In addition, Klan excesses began to take their toll. There was a cry of outrage when the Exalted Cyclops of Portland told an audience in Salem: "The only way to cure a Catholic is to kill him."

The citizens of Oregon had been deluded for a time by Klan oratory, but they had too much common sense and too much decency to sanction the killing of a man for his religious beliefs. The *Capitol Journal* now ran a series of exposés on the Klan. Other papers, so long silent, followed suit. Many ministers, aroused by the antagonisms the Klan was creating in their own congregations, began to denounce the hooded order. The tide turned swiftly. The Klan, which at its peak probably had 25,000 members in the state, saw its power swept away as if carried out to sea by the Columbia River in flood. In the elections of 1924, Klan-supported candidates lost everywhere. The Klan as a force was dead in Oregon.

CHAPTER

10

HIGH TIDE IN INDIANA

THE Klan madness reached its peak in Indiana and in the career of its Grand Dragon, D. C. Stephenson, one of the plotters who had sold "Colonel" Simmons on accepting his own eclipse. Shrewd and ambitious, with his eyes set on the White House, Stephenson built the Indiana Klan into such a powerhouse that it practically owned the entire state.

Indiana was ripe for the kind of demagoguery the Klan practiced. A crossroads state of the Midwest, wedged in between Ohio on one side and Illinois on the other, it was crisscrossed by rum runners plying their trade from the Great Lakes to the big cities, Chicago and St. Louis. Inevitably, it was a badly corrupted state. Everything was for sale: whiskey, women, police, and public officials.

It would have been hard to find richer soil for the flourishing of the Klan's version of 100 percent Americanism. Indiana had a host of native-born demons to be fought, and what it didn't have, the Klan could easily manufacture.

The Klan made its first foray into Indiana in 1920, but its leadership at the beginning was inept. Then Stephenson took control, and things began to happen.

Daniel Clarke Stephenson had been born in Texas in 1891. An elementary school dropout, he drifted from job to job, and when the United States entered World War I, he joined the army. He came out a lieutenant, a rank that Klan propaganda would later elevate to "major."

Stephenson settled in Evansville in 1920 and went into the coal business. He also became extremely active in veterans' organizations. He had all the gifts of a snake-oil salesman. His figure was inclined to pudginess, a drawback that he concealed under well-tailored, conservative suits. In manner, he could be all things to all men. He had the folksy touch on the one hand and the flowery bombast of the political orator on the other.

In 1922, Stephenson took control of the Klan in Evansville, and in a few months, he recruited 5,000 followers. He began to live in style. When he went to Atlanta for the first great Klonvokation—and, incidentally, the overthrow of Simmons—he traveled by private railway car. He returned with his power ratified over Klan activities in twenty-two northern and midwestern states.

Now he began to build a political empire. He wanted numbers, and he didn't care about the character of the joiners. Numbers meant power, and Stephenson wanted power. Meetings, parades, field days were held. Klansmen and their affiliates, Ladies of the Golden Mask, turned out by the tens of thousands and the scores of thousands. The constant, ongoing Klan circus was soon swinging the whole state of Indiana by the tail.

As happened everywhere the Klan operated, fanatical rabble-rousers soon whipped the populace into a frenzy about the dangers posed by Catholicism and the Pope. Only about thirteen out of every one hundred residents of Indiana were either black or Catholic; that fact made no difference to Klan orators. Their spiels turned nonexistent ghosts into menacing reality.

Indiana, of course, was largely fundamentalist Protestant country, and preachers of the old-time religion had long thundered to their flocks about the papal threat. So they had created a mental and emotional climate that led Hoosiers by the thousands to swallow whole the most preposterous Klan claptrap.

Typical was what happened in North Manchester, where a Klan lecturer roused his audience to heights of irrationality by declaiming against the Pope: "He may even be on the northbound train tomorrow! He may! He may! Be warned! Prepare! America is for Americans! Search everywhere for hidden enemies, vipers at the heart's blood of our sacred Republic! Watch the trains!"

So exhorted, a thousand residents of North Manchester turned out to meet the next northbound train to Chicago. Just one passenger alighted. He was instantly mobbed. The poor man, it turned out, was only a ladies' corset salesman, not the Pope, but he had the devil's own time convincing the aroused Klansmen and their followers that he was not the Pope in disguise. Finally released, he was put on the next train out of town.

This was only one example of the insanity that swept the state. Sheeted men marched in torchlit nights through Indiana towns in seemingly endless columns. Drums rolled, horses pranced, crosses burned. Down Kokomo's Main Street, a huge American flag, stretching from curb to curb, was paraded by Klansmen gathering contributions for a new hospital so that 100 percent Americans would not have to be treated by Catholic nuns.

The fever built to a frenzied pitch in July, 1923, when Stephenson was to be inaugurated Grand Dragon. Imperial Wizard Hiram Evans came up from Atlanta for the ceremony. More than 100,000 Klansmen gathered in Kokomo's Melfalfa Park. Bands played. Ministers flayed Catholics and the Devil. Evans gave his "Back to the Constitution" speech. And families lunched at long rows of tables.

Finally, an airplane appeared from the south. It circled low above the mob of Klansmen and landed in a nearby meadow. Down from the rear cockpit stepped Stephenson, clad in his purple silken robe. He was escorted to the speakers' platform, raised his hands to quiet the crowd, and launched into his best snake-oil speech.

"My worthy subjects, citizens of the Invisible Empire, Klansmen all—greetings," he began. "It grieves me to be late. The President of the United States kept me unduly long, counseling upon vital matters of state. Only my pleas that this is the time and place of my coronation obtained for me surcease from his prayers for guidance."

Apparently, not a single Klansman doubted that this was the truth, for the throng went into a kind of religious ecstasy when Stephenson was crowned after a speech calling for "straight Americanism." As he turned to leave the rally, a shower of coins, rings, charms, and pocketbooks fell about his feet. All tributes to the new Messiah of the Klan, without whose advice the President of the United States was helpless.

This tempestuous outpouring of feeling and the enormous size of the crowd must have made an impression on Imperial Wizard Evans. Perhaps he felt the hot breath of a rival breathing down his neck. In any event, it soon became clear that Evans and Stephenson were on a collision course.

Stephenson attended a secret strategy meeting the Imperial Wizard held in the Willard Hotel in Washington and came away disenchanted. He saw in the Klan a movement that could be welded into a great political force that would take control of the nation. Evans and his southern contingent, Stephenson thought, were regionally narrow in their viewpoint. They lacked vision. And they seemed preoccupied with the multiple legal entanglements resulting from the ousters of Clarke and Simmons.

The breach between Evans and Stephenson grew during the summer of 1923. They conferred in Cincinnati and aboard Stephenson's new yacht on Lake Huron. Evans kept talking about the lawsuits, and he sometimes dropped dark hints about violence and ensnarement to rid himself of unwanted rivals. Stephenson may well have thought the veiled threat was aimed at him.

Not a sensitive man, he was still a highly intelligent and capable one, and he must have realized that no one was more vulnerable than he to charges related to personal conduct. The truth was that Stephenson had two unquenchable appetites: one for whiskey, one for women. He and his close aides cut a wide swath that led through country roadhouses and hotel rooms. And his own new home in Indianapolis was known throughout the state as what, in later times, would be called "a swinging place."

With Evans apparently pressuring, a series of intricate maneuvers took place. Only a few months after his triumphal inauguration, Stephenson resigned his post as Grand Dragon. He retained his Klan membership, however, and he devoted the next months to building up his strength within the organization. By May, 1924, he felt he was strong enough to defy Evans and national headquarters in Atlanta. So he called a convention of his own followers and was elected Grand Dragon of the now independent Indiana Klan.

Evans responded by compiling a list of Stephenson's drunken misdeeds. This evidence was presented to Stephenson's home Klan in Evansville, and this Klavern obeyed Evans and obediently banished its former leader. Stephenson promptly sued Evans and Evans's hand-picked Grand Dragon, Walter Bossert, charging libel. (Klan leaders, it seemed, were always quarreling over power and the spoils that went with it, like dogs snarling over a juicy bone, and these quarrels always ended in lawsuits that split and discredited the Klan.) In this instance, Stephenson had hardly filed his suit when his yacht was mysteriously blown up in the harbor of Toledo. Though he lacked proof of the identity of the dynamiter, Stephenson had no doubt about who was responsible, and he added to his lawsuit additional charges against Evans and Bossert. At the same time, he denounced them as "yellow-livered southerners who hate everything that is pure throughout the state of Indiana."

Despite this cat-spitting warfare within the brotherhood, the quarreling factions managed to get together long enouth to seize control of Indiana in the election of 1924. They might not have cooperated so well had not the Democrats presented them with a rich opportunity. The Democratic governor, convicted of mail fraud, had been sent to the federal penitentiary in Atlanta. Other Democratic officeholders had been discredited by liquor and gambling scandals.

As a result, the Republican state convention more resembled a Klan Klonvokation than the gathering of a political party. Stephenson was everywhere on the floor. The Republican candidates selected to run against the Democrats in November were all his choices. Stephenson's man was elected governor. The Klan won control of the state legislature. In contests for local offices, it swept the board, electing sheriffs, court officials, district attorneys, school boards, most of the mayors. The new mayor of Indianapolis owed Stephenson so much that he agreed to consult the Klan leader on all civic and police appointments.

Stephenson was riding the crest of power. Still a young man in his thirties, he looked forward to an even more brilliant future. The U. S. senator from Indiana was ailing. When he went to his final reward, Stephenson expected to replace him. Then, with the national spotlight upon him, with the Klan legions behind him, he might reach for the White House in 1928. It did not seem impossible.

But such visions have a way of fading in politics. There are too many rivals with similar desires; there are too many chances, too many stumbling blocks, that can undo a man in his race to the summit. Then, too, there are those who, having acquired power, misuse power and so lay themselves open to attack by their enemies. Stephenson was just such a man.

The first roadblock Stephenson encountered was in the lower house of the state legislature. True, the Klan ruled it, but these Klansmen were for the most part followers of the Evans-Bossert faction. They did not belong to Stephenson, and so Stephenson soon discovered that, although he controlled the governor and the state senate, he could not get the legislation he wanted enacted into law. The opposing Klan faction in the lower house balked at every turn.

At the same time, the measures that the Evans-Bossert faction wanted would pass the lower house—and then die quietly in the Stephenson-controlled Senate. It was a stalemate, with the rival Klan factions cutting each other's throats.

One of the lower house bills that Stephenson killed brought him to disaster. It was a thing so minor that it would seem impossible at first glance that calamity could result from it. The bill would have abolished a minor job in the office of the state superintendent of public instruction. The job was held by short, plumpish, twenty-eight-year-old Madge Oberholtzer. After Stephenson saved her job for her, he began taking her out.

Madge was certainly no beauty, but "the old man," as Stephenson was called by his followers, had an eye for almost any woman. Perhaps Madge was just young enough and attractive enough to interest him. And he was such a powerful man that Madge felt flattered when he dated her. So an emotional powder train was set.

Returning home from a date with another man early one night in March, 1925, Madge found that Stephenson had been telephoning her and wanted her to call him back. She did. He sent one of his bodyguards to escort her to the mansion. There she found that Stephenson had been drinking heavily. She later charged that he "forced" her to drink with him. Then, while intoxicated, she was hustled by Stephenson and his bodyguards into his private drawing room on a train bound for Chicago.

There he attacked her. Madge and Stephenson left the train in the morning at Hammond, on the Indiana side of the state line. Had they crossed the state line, Stephenson would have been liable to prosecution under the federal Mann Act, just as Edward Clarke had been earlier.

Too canny to leave himself open to such a charge, Stephenson took Madge to a hotel to wait for his car which, he said, was being driven up from Indianapolis. Pretending that she wanted to buy a hat, Madge got some money from him. With it, she purchased, not a hat, but poison. This she drank.

Thoroughly frightened, Stephenson offered to take her to a hospital if she would marry him. In disgust, she refused. Stephenson's car arrived, and the drive back to Indianapolis began. Madge was in agony, but Stephenson refused to stop and find a doctor for her. Arriving in Indianapolis, Stephenson hid her away for another day in the loft apartment over his garage. He continued to plead with her to marry him, but time and again she refused. Thwarted, Stephenson finally had his men drive Madge to her home. She died several weeks later, and her father charged Stephenson with murder.

When the case went to trial, the defense tried to blacken Madge's character and to pick at discrepancies in her deathbed statement. The defense also relied heavily on the argument that Stephenson hadn't killed Madge; she had taken the poison and killed herself. Stephenson did not take the stand in his own defense. It seems that Stephenson, who had called himself "the law" in Indiana, was confident that so many owed him so much that nothing could happen to him. He was wrong. He was convicted, sentenced, and sent to the state penitentiary.

The scandal marked the beginning of the end for the Klan in Indiana, a state that the hooded order had held as virtually its private fief. The Evans faction was ecstatic at the downfall of Stephenson, but the quarreling and squabbling within the Klan continued. Klan candidates still did fairly well in the municipal elections in 1925, but the statewide revulsion caused by the Stephenson affair continued to erode the order's strength.

Stephenson had counted confidently on receiving a pardon from his friend, Governor Ed Jackson, but Jackson, recognizing the public temper, was not willing to commit political suicide by springing his benefactor from prison. When it became apparent to Stephenson that he was not going to be released, he turned to vengeance. He passed the word to his aides to release the contents of the "little black box" in which he had kept a record of all the deals he made when he wielded statewide power.

The scandal that erupted spelled the death knell of the Klan in Indiana. One of Stephenson's documents proved especially embarrassing to Governor Jackson. It was a canceled check showing that the governor had received $2,500 from Stephenson. Trapped, the governor came up with an explanation no discredited politician had ever thought of before. It is almost standard operating procedure in such cases for the accused politico to name an associate whose testimony would clear him—but, unfortunately, the associate is conveniently dead. Governor Jackson went this ploy one better. He called to his defense a horse. He had, he said, sold the horse to Stephenson for $2,500; that was what the check represented—payment for the horse. But, unfortunately, the horse had choked to death on a corncob.

The Klan in Indiana choked to death on the revelations that came tumbling out of Stephenson's little black box. A score of prominent Republicans wound up behind bars. The party chairman in the state was convicted of violating the banking laws. Graft prosecutions snared many. Governor Jackson was tried for attempting to bribe his predecessor, and he and several other party leaders were saved only because so much time had elapsed that the statute of limitations (a law providing that a criminal charge must be brought within a certain number of years) had run out, making it impossible to prosecute them.

Through all the furor, Stephenson remained in prison. He was not released until 1956, thirty-one years later; by that time, hardly anyone remembered who he was or what he had been.

CHAPTER

11

COLLAPSE

THE Ku Klux Klan, which had seemed to be sweeping all before it in the early 1920s, collapsed like a pricked balloon and vanished from the American scene even more swiftly than it had risen. In 1924, it wielded awesome power; by 1928, it was virtually nothing.

The experiences in Oregon and Indiana were matched in other states across the nation. Politicians who had not dared speak out against the hooded order suddenly found it safe to denounce it. Newspapers that had kept silent when the Klan was a menace began to attack it. Ministers who had embraced it, or at least tolerated it, suddenly thundered from their pulpits with the voice of the Lord. The American people returned to their senses and abandoned the Klan.

What is the explanation for this drastic turnaround in a few brief years?

There were many reasons for the sudden eclipse of the Klan. For one thing, the movement had no solid base, no ideals, no positive program. It depended solely on negatives. Its appeal was to fanatic emotion, and emotion can be sustained at a fevered pitch for only a limited amount of time. The Klan appealed to the basest impulses of the American spirit. It whipped up hate based on bigotry. Its "menaces" were the Catholic church, blacks, Jews, and immigrating foreigners. But when these "menaces" failed to menace, the Klan was left with ghosts of its own creation. The blacks did not revolt in the South; it became obvious that the Pope was not going to tunnel into the White House. And so the Klan was left empty-handed.

Even more devastating, perhaps, were the disclosures that resulted from the constant wrangling among the Klan leadership. Stephenson's little black box in Indiana had disgorged details about briberies and payoffs that disillusioned all but the most stupid. That was only one of many such revelations. It became obvious that Imperial Wizards and their principal followers had been more interested in lining their own pockets than in promoting noble ideas. The lawsuits in which they became entangled as they quarreled over the spoils were exercises in self-exposure. The American public became aware of the extent of the Klan's brutalities. It also recognized the hypocrisy of an organization that preached holiness and then besmirched itself with the most unholy deeds. The effect was doubly devastating.

The swift revulsion that spelled the doom of the Klan is amazing when one considers the extent of its power and the depth of its fall. In its heyday, between 1920 and 1925, the Klan had some two million members and collected an estimated $40 million in revenue. Some of these millions of dollars were raised for specific projects that were never built because too much money stuck to the fingers of greedy Klan officials. By 1929, disillusionment within the ranks of the Klan was almost complete. The Klan vanished from the northern, midwestern, and western states and was left with only a few thousand followers in its historic stronghold in the Deep South.

Ironically, its collapse came just at a time when the Klan might have capitalized on claims of victory. In 1924, a new and more stringent immigration act was passed, severely limiting the number of foreigners who could be admitted into the United States each year. In 1928, the Democrats nominated New York's genial Al Smith, a Catholic, for the presidency, and the Klan had its desired "Catholic menace" to combat. It raged against "priest rule," held bonfire rallies and pamphleteered in more than twenty states. When Smith was crushed by Herbert Hoover in a landslide vote, the Invisible Empire boasted that it had nailed "Smith's political hide to the Klan's barn door." But few believed it. The consensus was that Hoover's triumph resulted from his reputation as a great engineer and administrator, aided by the legacy of the wild prosperity of the Roaring Twenties that President Calvin Coolidge had left him.

The Klan's claims of victory had an especially hollow ring and deceived almost no one, coming as they did on the heels of one of its worst exposures. In 1927, a group of rebellious western Klansmen, disgusted with top-level management and encouraged by their ministers, withdrew from the order. Imperial Wizard Hiram Evans sued them for $100,000 in damages. He had two objectives: to get his hands on their regalia and treasury, and to serve a warning on any other like-minded Klaverns that he could crack down upon them if they tried to leave the Invisible Empire.

This suit by Evans was the final blow to the Klan. It was not a criminal case, but an equity one, that is an appeal for justice in a case not covered by law. The defending Klansmen became in effect the plaintiffs. They turned the case around by contending that the national Klan came into court with sullied hands and reputation—and so had no right to claim anything.

For days, newspaper headlines featured the sensational disclosures poured out in this courtroom battle. Klan secrets, Klan intrigues, Klan brutalities and murders—all were spread on the public record in a seemingly endless stream.

D. C. Stephenson sent an affidavit from Michigan City Penitentiary describing Klan outrages in Indiana. "Colonel" Simmons testified about the manner in which he had been betrayed in the grubby struggle for Klan power and wealth. Witnesses told of the Klan's kidnapping of a small girl from her grandparents' home in Pittsburgh. Others testified that a Colorado Klansman had been beaten to death when he tried to leave the order. The court record became filled with descriptions of whippings, floggings, and murders. One horror story that capped all others dealt with a man in Terrell, Texas, who was doused with oil and burned to death in the presence of several hundred Klansmen. The details were so overwhelming and so disgusting that the judge hearing the case, in a furious decision, threw out Hiram Evans's suit and denounced the Klan for the monster it was.

Despite such disclosures, there was never an accurate tally of the number of atrocities the Klan had committed. Many victims of its floggings and its tar-and-feathering parties naturally fled and kept silent, fearing that even worse might happen to them if they spoke out. Thus, the only indication comes from the scattered incidents that did come to light in a number of states.

The evidence indicated that, in Texas and Oklahoma alone, there had been more than one thousand assault cases. There had been more than one hundred in the states of Florida, Georgia, and Alabama; more than a score in the North Carolina Piedmont region. California, Oregon, Arizona, and the midwestern and mountain states had all had their bloody incidents.

The impact that such disclosures made upon the public consciousness was bad enough for the Klan but less disastrous than the sensations stirred up by individual, dramatic stories. In the end, the Klan was stripped of its hooded masks and white sheets, and the skeleton within was exposed to the gaze of all Americans. Once they saw and recognized the Klan for what it was, the people of the nation turned from it as if fleeing from the Devil against whom the Klan had preached.

CHAPTER

12

DEPRESSION DOLDRUMS

THE years of the Great Depression were a bleak time for the Ku Klux Klan. Just as it had had no positive program in the years of its power from 1920 to 1925, so it had nothing to offer a public concerned with the collapse of virtually the entire American economy. With banks failing, with millions upon millions unemployed, with factories idle and all business life at a standstill, the Klan's anti-Catholic, anti-Semitic, and antiblack rhetoric seemed unrealistic. It had nothing to do with the great issues of the day.

This does not mean that the Klan was dead. The history of the Klan shows that it never dies. It fades away into obscurity at times, but it maintains a half-life under the surface of American society. Then, when the time is right, when issues appealing to deep wells of prejudice arise, the Klan revives and rides again with all of its old brutality and hatred.

The decade of the 1930s was one of the submerged and waiting-for-an-issue periods for the Klan. Its various Klaverns, scattered across the nation, still had perhaps 100,000 members. There were pockets of the Invisible Empire in New Jersey, New York, Pennsylvania, Michigan, Ohio, Illinois, Kentucky, California, and Virginia. But its greatest strength was in the South, its birthplace, especially in the states of Georgia and Florida.

Out of tune with the times, Klansmen devoted themselves to fraternal and social functions. Klaverns visited Klaverns, held occasional rallies, burned a few crosses. But it was all pretty tame.

Even as the Klan waited for an issue, it continued to appeal to passion and tried to whip up racial hatreds. James Colescott, Ohio's Grand Dragon and a rising power in the Klan, ordered his followers to avoid "lawless" unemployment demonstrations. An official of the Akron Klavern denounced those who took part in a hunger march on the state capital as "Negroes, Hunks, Dagos, and all the rest of the scum of Europe's slums."

The Klan, it seemed, was not only violent in action, but violent in language. It could not discuss even such vital issues of the day as unemployment and hunger marches without descending into name-calling.

Strangely, the Klan at first supported Franklin D. Roosevelt for the presidency in 1932. Roosevelt's many visits to a health spa in Warm Springs, Georgia, where he struggled to recover from crippling polio, had made him a popular figure in the South. But then the Klan, to its horror, discovered that Roosevelt had chosen for his campaign manager James A. Farley, of New York, *a Catholic.*

Klan support turned quickly into bitter opposition. When Roosevelt was elected and made Farley postmaster general, the Klan promptly blasted his administration for bringing "too many Jews and Catholics" to Washington. It was only a short mental jump from this to raising the communist issue. Soon the Klan was attacking Roosevelt's New Deal for "having honeycombed Washington with communists." At an Annapolis rally, more than one thousand Klansmen and their women were told that a wave of communism was sweeping the nation and that the depression would not be ended until there was a return to "fundamental principles." In Westchester County, New York, Klan orators praised the new German führer, Adolf Hitler, and denounced the "communism of FDR and the Jews."

In this fashion, by a process of gradual drift, the Klan found what it always had to have—a menace. The new menace was communism as personified in the actions of Roosevelt's New Deal. Imperial Wizard Hiram Evans and his aides saw communists everywhere—in the schools, in the federal administration, in the Supreme Court. Given this bias, it was almost inevitable that the Klan, in the late 1930s, would become entangled with the German-American Bund.

The Bund was an American front organization for Hitler's Nazi party. Its program of racial hate fit nicely into the Klan's own bigotry. Klan leaders and Bund and openly Nazi followers met on friendly terms, and in one New Jersey gathering, the Klan and the Bund joined forces openly.

The rally was held on August 18, 1940, at the Bund's Camp Norland near Andover, New Jersey. Several hundred robed Klansmen were present. Arthur H. Bell, a Bloomfield lawyer who had led the New Jersey Klan in the 1920s, attacked the singing of "God Bless America." He called it a Semitic song fit to be sung only in Bowery taverns and brothels.

Edward James Smythe, head of the Protestant War Veterans and organizer of the meeting, went further. He praised Bund Leader Fritz Kuhn. In reply, the Camp Norland Bund director referred "to the common bond between us" and added, "The principles of the Bund and the principles of the Klan are the same."

The rally ended with a Klan wedding performed under the glare of a fiery cross. Neighborhood residents gathered outside the fenced-in camp and began to shout, "Put Hitler on the cross." When they then started to sing "The Star-Spangled Banner," the Bund band struck up so loudly that it drowned them out.

The public reaction to this display of fraternity was so hostile that the Klan backtracked hastily. It repudiated the meeting and ousted Arthur Bell and the Rev. A. M. Young, the New Jersey Klan secretary. And the southern wing of the Klan, through its publication, *The Fiery Cross*, attacked the Bund.

Though the approach of World War II made it inadvisable for the Klan to associate openly with the Bund, the beliefs and aims of the two organizations were similar. Indeed, some of the Bund leaders came out of the old 1920s Klan movement, and, in the decades ahead, Nazis and Klansmen often demonstrated their compatibility.

One strong theme ran through the continuing Klan movement in the South: resistance to any change in the social structure. The resistance had many facets. The black must be kept in his place and scared away from the voting booth. Union organizers must be harassed, beaten, driven out. Any attempt to organize labor to get better working conditions or higher wages was viewed by the Klan as a socialistic or communistic tactic—and the Klan was opposed to all such "foreign isms."

These attitudes were expressed most forcibly in Florida, where the Klan was strongest. It was estimated to have 30,000 members there despite the decline of the national organization, and its night riders spread terror through many sections of the state.

"The CIO [Congress of Industrial Organizations, a federation of labor unions, led by Walter Reuther] is a subversive, radical, Red organization, and we'll fight fire with fire," one Klan leader proclaimed.

It was no idle threat. In the citrus groves of Florida, owners opposed to paying higher wages and the Klan, seeing Red, were of one mind. Unions attempting to organize the workers must be balked by any means, even the most violent. One organizer working among the citrus laborers in Lakeland got a call for help in the night, responded to it—and was never seen again. Klansmen sometimes boasted about the bodies that had been dumped in swamps and in abandoned, water-filled phosphate mines.

One outrage perpetrated by the Klan attracted national attention. A group called the Modern Democrats, led largely by socialists, attempted to mount a reform movement to clean up Tampa's city government, riddled as it was with vice and political spoils. One might have thought the Klan, which had always professed to be the foe of corruption, would at least have tolerated such a movement. But, no, to the Klan, the Modern Democrats were dangerous radicals to be eliminated by any means, even the most inhuman.

The Klan had a strong following among city employees, especially among firemen and policemen—a tie with officialdom that has endured in the South for decades and has often prevented justice from being done. In Tampa, a fireman joined the Modern Democrats as a spy, keeping the police informed of the group's intentions. The result: police raided a meeting of the reformers, arrested and questioned several—and then turned them over to Klan floggers. With one victim, Joseph Shoemaker, the Klan went further. He was brutally murdered.

The death of Shoemaker caused a national outburst of indignation. The mayor and board of aldermen of Tampa ordered an investigation. The American Civil Liberties Union, labor groups, the American Legion, and the Veterans of Foreign Wars all condemned the brutality. A National Committee for the Defense of Civil Rights was organized in Tampa, headed by the much-respected socialist leader Norman Thomas. The mayor, at the request of the Tampa Ministerial Association, called for a period of public mourning. Ministers from all the major Protestant faiths participated. Then what happened?

The Tampa chief of police investigated and found all his men innocent. None of them had had anything to do with the incident. A grand jury took a different view. It indicted several officers, including Chief Tittsworth himself.

Now the forces of repression rallied. The existing order must be upheld, regardless of the treatment of Shoemaker. Local cigar manufacturers put up bail for the accused; high-priced lawyers were engaged to defend them. Governor Eugene Talmadge's Georgia Veterans' Bureau got into the act, trading charges with Norman Thomas. The accused murderers were wrapped in the mantle of patriotism; those who sought justice, like Norman Thomas, were denounced as communists. In the midst of the public uproar, a crucial prosecution witness mysteriously "committed suicide."

Despite damaging testimony from the Tampa chief of detectives and some of the more decent policemen on the force, the presiding judge at the trial directed a verdict of acquittal for Tittsworth and another defendant. The remaining defendants went free after two trials and appeals, with the Florida court holding that kidnapping meant only "intent to secretly confine." What had happened to Shoemaker obviously had not disturbed the consciences of the old-line power brokers in Florida.

The Shoemaker case was an especially appalling example, but it was typical of what happened time and again throughout the South. As unions organized and gained strength during the Roosevelt era, the Klan found its new menace. It still used its muscle to keep blacks away from the polls, but Imperial Wizard Evans sent out instructions to soft-pedal the anti-Catholic and anti-Semitic issues that had been the Klan's basic tenets. Now the emphasis was to be placed on "communist union organizers" who were seeking to undermine the social order of the South and bring on "industrial war."

The antiunion effort was organized by James Colescott, a former veterinarian from Terre Haute, Indiana, who had been one of D. C. Stephenson's lieutenants in the Klan's glory days. Colescott had been brought to Atlanta by Imperial Wizard Evans to be chief of staff. The interests of the Klan and the white business leadership of the South now merged beautifully, and the Klan found itself being liberally financed. It moved into new headquarters, dug out old membership lists, and launched a new recruiting campaign.

With the Klan apparently reviving, Imperial Wizard Evans stumbled. His loud protestations that the Klan was no longer anti-Catholic were taken up by the Catholics. In January, 1939, they invited Evans to attend the dedication of the Catholic Cathedral of Christ the King, located on the grounds of the Klan's old, white-pillared Imperial Palace. The property had been sold to an insurance company, which, in turn, had sold it to the Catholic church. The church's invitation put Evans on the spot, but he decided he had no choice. He attended the dedication ceremony.

There was an instant upheaval among rank-and-file Klansmen. It might be all right to *say* the Klan should be more tolerant of Catholics, but to associate publicly with the infidels was just too much! The uproar became so vociferous that Hiram Evans had to step down. On June 10, 1939, he surrendered his post as Imperial Wizard after nearly seventeen years, and James Colescott succeeded him.

CHAPTER 13

THE KLAN SPLINTERS

JAMES Colescott donned the robes of Imperial Wizard at a time when the Klan seemed irrelevant to the larger events happening in the world. These were the days of World War II, and the attention of the American people was focused on developments on far-off battlefields in Europe and the Pacific, not on the rantings of the Ku Klux Klan.

A short, stocky man, Colescott was bald and round-faced. He did not have the presence or the oratorical flourishes of "Colonel" Simmons, nor was he the glad-hander that Hiram Evans had been. He was, however, a good organizer and hard worker, and he did his best to keep alive the flagging Klan movement.

He toured the North, the Midwest, and Florida. The Michigan Klan pushed recruitment among the blue-collar automobile workers of Detroit, aided by a weekly radio program. Colescott found, however, that southern Indiana, once a hotbed of Klan activity, had turned decidely cool to the Klan, the result of the "Stephenson affair." Only in the South did Colescott find the same old-time fervor; only in the South did the Klans ride at night in their old terroristic fashion.

Black voters were threatened and kept away from the polls in Miami and in Greenville, South Carolina. In addition to the racial issue, the Klan kept playing on its new theme that any labor union activity was equivalent to communism. This tactic was especially effective in South Carolina, where organized labor had been growing.

Colescott, like a slippery politician, tried to have it both ways. Publicly, he proclaimed that the Klan was not antiunion, not opposed to the CIO. But Klan publications and Klan activity contradicted his protestations. One headline in *The Fiery Cross* read: CIO WANTS BLACKS AND WHITES ON SAME LEVEL. The article underneath charged that the CIO was a communist organization trying to deceive people into thinking it was a labor union.

This Klan union-busting activity was heartily supported by southern businessmen. Press reports quoted them as backing the Klan's attempt to run the CIO out of the South. There were a lot of good men, said the business leaders, who felt just the way they did. This linkage of the Klan and prominent southerners was to have far-reaching effects, for in the postwar era the combined activity of the two partners was to play a major role in altering the economy of the nation. Some northern manufacturing cities were to become virtual ghost towns as the large textile mills on which they had depended for employment moved to the South, where labor was unorganized—and cheap.

The Klan was a major force in keeping things that way. It was especially strong in the western textile-manufacturing counties of Anderson and Greenville in South Carolina. In Anderson, night riders flogged both union organizers and some of the unorganized workers whom they suspected or whose moral conduct they questioned. In Greenville, armed Klansmen twice raided the National Youth Administration camp. They robbed and beat up some of the young blacks in the camp and tacked up a sign reading: NIGGERS, YOUR PLACE IS IN THE COTTON PATCH. Blacks were openly assaulted with the cooperation of the Klan's brothers in uniform—the local police. The joint effort crushed the campaign to register black voters.

Georgia was, if possible, even worse than South Carolina. It possessed, however, one powerful voice of reason that drove Klansmen almost up the wall. The voice belonged to Ralph McGill, the courageous editor of the Atlanta *Constitution*. McGill fought the Klan relentlessly, and Klansmen retaliated by donning their hoods and robes and demonstrating in front of the Atlanta *Constitution* building.

In the open country outside Atlanta, the Klan did not confine itself to demonstrations. There night riders were almost constantly ranging across the countryside, using terror to curb the CIO's organizing drives and to keep black voters from the polls. As was often the case when Klansmen began flogging, they developed such a thirst for the bloody exercise that they often lashed indiscriminately.

An unfortunate East Point barber, who liked his bottle, became one such victim. He was seized by Klansmen one dark night in March, 1940, flogged into unconsciousness and left to die in the frost-covered woods. If this had happened to a black, Georgia probably would not have been unduly disturbed, but the victim in this case was a white barber whose only offense was his fondness for liquor. The scandal could not be hushed up, and a grand jury was impaneled to investigate the Klan's activities.

Assistant Attorney General Daniel Duke, a dynamic young lawyer, handled the probe. Under his guidance, the grand jury concluded that some fifty other Georgians had been worked over by the Klan in the preceding two years. The victims included the white owner of a Negro theater in Decatur, a fundamentalist minister, and a young Atlanta couple who had been beaten to death in a lovers' lane. Eight of the sadistic floggers, including several deputy sheriffs, were indicted, tried, convicted, and sent to prison. Then the Klan began a campaign to get one of its favorite governors, Eugene Talmadge, to grant the floggers executive clemency.

Daniel Duke, furious, opposed their release from prison. *Life* magazine gave this vivid picture of the confrontation between the young prosecutor and the governor:

"On a table in front of Governor Eugene Talmadge were two leather man whips that might have come straight from a Gestapo cellar in Poland. Also on the table were clemency petitions for...Ku Klux Klansmen now in prison for flogging pro-union mill workers. Assistant Solicitor Dan Duke, fighting the petitions, shook a whip in the Governor's face and shouted: 'These are whips you could kill a bull elephant with.' Gene Talmadge...stared straight at the whip. Then he announced that he was sorry for the floggers, would take their pleas under consideration. He recalled that he had once helped flog a Negro himself. 'I wasn't in such bad company,' he said. 'The Apostle Paul was a flogger in his life, then confessed, reformed, and became one of the greatest of the Christian Church. That proves to me that good people can be misguided to do bad things.'"

After the Japanese attack on Pearl Harbor, Duke left to join the marines, and Governor Talmadge, ignoring newspaper and church protests, pardoned the floggers.

By so doing, he set a significant precedent. It was a pattern that was to be repeated many times in the 1950s and 1960s. Each time a racially explosive issue arose, the Klan gathered strength and resorted to its favorite tactics: floggings and murder. In the 1950s, passions boiled over after the U.S. Supreme Court ordered school desegration; in the 1960s, the same thing happened when civil rights workers mounted a massive campaign to register black voters. When murder followed, southern white officialdom often acted very much as had Governor Talmadge, banding together to protect the murderers.

Before these two decades of turmoil, the Klan had gone through a period of eclipse. The 1940s, with their emphasis on world war, were a trying time for an organization that needed to ride against a domestic menace. And the Roosevelt and Truman administrations in Washington were not inclined to blink at atrocities like those Daniel Duke had exposed.

The U. S. Bureau of Internal Revenue, the same federal agency that had brought down the murderous underworld czar, Al Capone, began looking into the affairs of the Klan. In 1944, it delivered a crushing blow. It filed a lien against the Invisible Empire for $685,000 in taxes it had failed to pay in the halcyon days of the 1920s. It was a body blow that spelled the death knell of the Klan as it was then constituted.

Imperial Wizard Colescott was bitter. In retirement in Miami, he later exploded: "It was that nigger-lover Roosevelt and that Jew Morgenthau who was his Secretary of Treasury who did it! I was sitting in my office in the Imperial Palace in Atlanta one day, just as pretty as you please, when the Revenurs (sic) knocked on my door and said they had come to collect three-quarters of a million dollars that the government just figured out the Klan owed as taxes earned in the 1920s... We had to sell our assets and go out of business. Maybe the Government can make something of the Klan—I never could."

The Treasury Department's action had lopped off the head of the octopus. The main organization had been destroyed, but a lot of its tentacles were still quivering and alive. The Klan became splintered into local Klaverns and, in time, into a number of competing Klans. But the purposes of all remained essentially the same. The campaigns of racial bigotry, intolerance, and violence continued.

CHAPTER 14

AFTER Internal Revenue made the Invisible Empire truly invisible, there was a free-for-all struggle to pick up the shattered pieces. Almost any hate-monger with a little bit of leadership ability could set up his own Klan and rally a number of night riders bent on mischief.

One of the first of the new organizers was Dr. Samuel Green, a fifty-five-year-old Atlanta obstetrician. Green, who had been a Klansman since the early 1920s, obtained some of the old Klan's application blanks and stamped across them the name of his new order: THE ASSOCIATION OF GEORGIA KLANS. And in October, 1946, he led his followers up Stone Mountain. There they lighted the first cross that had been burned on the summit since Pearl Harbor.

Klaverns began to spring up all over the South. Their membership was often small, but their voices were loud and shrill. The federal movement for a fair employment act to prevent job discrimination on the basis of race, color, or religion drove these fanatics to new depths of vituperation and violence.

A special effort was made to incite returning servicemen to hate "the niggahs who got all the good jobs while you were in uniform." Grand Dragon Green told an interviewer, "I'll tell you this, no CIO or AFL carpetbagging organizers, or any other damned Yankees, are going to come into the South and tell southerners how to run either their business or their niggahs."

He added, "We won't tolerate any alliance between niggahs, Jews, Catholics, and labor organizers either."

All of the objects of Klan prejudice and hate were identified in that one sentence.

Green proved to be an able organizer on the Georgia scene. He got many law officers and city councilmen to join his Klan, giving his organization protection on the local level. He made a special mysterious drive to sign up cab drivers. "When the word comes, every cab in Atlanta will be needed," he told Atlanta Klavern No. 1 ominously. Just what "the word" was and what they would be "needed" for never became clear.

The Georgia Klan under Green played an important role in 1948, however. This was the year in which President Harry S. Truman ran for office. He had offended the South by his championship of fair employment, and so the Klan whooped it up for the Dixiecrat candidate, Strom Thurmond, splitting the Democratic vote in the once-solid South.

In Georgia, the Klan had a political interest even closer to its heart. It had worked hand-in-glove with Governor Eugene Talmadge, and in this year of 1948, Gene's son, Herman, was running for governor. Green's night-riding Klansmen so terrified blacks that they stayed away from the polls in droves, and Herman Talmadge, who was to go on to become a United States senator, won the Democratic gubernatorial nomination and the election. He showed his appreciation by appointing Green a lieutenant colonel and aide-de-camp on his staff.

Buoyed by this success, the Klan began to expand into neighboring states. The courageous Mississippi editor, Hodding Carter, wrote that the Klan was "sloshing over like an overfilled cesspool from its Georgia stronghold." Green claimed more than two hundred Klaverns were active in Georgia, South Carolina, Florida, Alabama, and Tennessee, but federal tax investigators estimated that the total number of Klansmen was not more than ten thousand. Other estimates placed the number at double that figure, still a small proportion of the population in the states involved.

In August, 1949, Grand Dragon Green was fatally stricken in the rose garden of his Atlanta home, and the leadership of the Klans became even more splintered. Despite their relatively small numbers and their divided leadership, the Klansmen were such terrorists that they caused havoc wherever they were established.

They burned crosses as warnings to their selected enemies. They fired bullets into the homes of unfriendly lawyers. They threatened newspaper editors in Gastonia, North Carolina, and Milledgeville, Georgia. Two Chattanooga men who refused to kneel before a blazing cross in Tennessee were severely flogged by Klansmen. The night riders turned Tennessee into a land of terror so that neighbor was afraid to visit neighbor after dark.

One of the most vicious leaders in this dark time was an Atlanta wholesale grocer named Tom Hamilton. Plump and bespectacled, he had been a member of Green's Association of Georgia Klans, and, after Green's death, he decided to strike out on his own. He moved to the little town of Leesburg in South Carolina and was soon doing such a prosperous Klan business that he gave up his wholesale grocery trade entirely. It was not long before the customary, brutal floggings began.

Men who drank too much, who beat their wives, who failed to attend church regularly, who ran around with other women—all were marked for punishment by Hamilton's self-appointed purists. All kinds of ruses were used to gain admittance to the homes of selected victims. A "motorist" whose car had broken down might come to the door seeking help; a passerby might ask to use the telephone. If doors were opened to such decoys, masked Klansmen flooded in, dragged out the occupants, and had themselves a flogging party. The terror became so widespread that homeowners bolted their doors at night and kept their shotguns handy. On the North Carolina side of the state line, the depredations became so bad that a sheriff reported, "My deputies are afraid to go to anybody's house at night to carry out even routine duties—people down here are in a mood to shoot first and ask questions afterwards."

Finally, in 1952, Hamilton's goons committed an act of savagery that did them in. Calling themselves the Southlands Sports Club of Fair Bluff, they pulled a man and woman out of bed and took them from North Carolina into South Carolina. There they lashed them. The self-appointed guardians of the moral order had made a strategic mistake, however, when they crossed the state line. This made their "sporting" performance a federal offense, and the Federal Bureau of Investigation stepped in. In a series of court cases, fifty-eight Klansmen were fined, and more than a score went to prison for an average of three years. Grand Dragon Hamilton himself drew a four-year sentence.

Such was the state of things in the South when the U. S. Supreme Court on May 17, 1954, outlawed school segregation. The decision triggered violence worse than anything that had gone before. New leaders of new Klans sprang up throughout the South, preaching the same old doctrine of racial hatred.

Eldon Edwards, a red-haired paint sprayer at General Motors' Fisher Body plant in Atlanta, took over the remnants of the departed Dr. Green's Associated Klans. Jesse B. Stoner set up shop in Atlanta. His partner was James Venable, owner of Stone Mountain. Stoner advocated elimination of the Jews and, when he was not working as a Klansman, headed the viciously anti-Semitic National States Right Party, which had adopted the SS symbol of Hitler's Nazis. Another of the new leaders was Asa "Ace" Carter, an Alabama farm boy who, after service in the navy, had worked as a radio announcer. He had been fired eventually for denouncing Jews on his broadcasts.

Ace's followers were the most militant of the lot. One of them leaped to the stage during a concert at the Birmingham Municipal Auditorium and assaulted Nat "King" Cole. In another case, four of Ace's goons drew twenty years in prison for kidnapping and assaulting a helpless black. When black coed Autherine Lucy was admitted to the University of Alabama, a contingent of Ace's roughnecks were in the Tuscaloosa mob that tried to stop her. Ace Carter's metoric career in the Klan ended in a blaze of gunfire. At a meeting of his Klavern, two members challenged Ace's dictatorial way of running things and tried to question him about what was happening to the group's finances. Ace wasn't a man to take such a challenge kindly. He simply drew the revolver he always carried strapped around his waist and shot both of his questioners. Fortunately, they recovered, and Ace was tried for attempted murder instead of murder. He was acquitted, but he was just about finished as a Klan leader.

As the struggle to keep the South's segregated way of life continued, some of the more cautious Southerners formed organizations less blackened by violence than the Klan. White Citizens' Councils sprang up, relying on economic and political pressures. They ran anti-Communist crusades and tried to attach the communist label to any politician who supported desegregation. This program dovetailed nicely with the Klan's propaganda while disassociating itself from the Klan's actions.

Those actions reached an unprecedented peak of violence. The record for the first four years after the Supreme Court's decision read like a battlefront report from a war zone. A 1959 study made by the Friends Service Committee, the National Council of Churches of Christ, and the Southern Regional Council showed this toll:

Six blacks killed.

Twenty-nine persons, eleven of them white, shot and wounded in racial incidents.

Forty-four persons beaten.

Five persons stabbed.

Thirty homes bombed. (In one bombing in Clinton, Tennessee, the blast was so severe that thirty additional homes were damaged; there were attempted fire bombings of five other homes.)

Eight homes burned.

Fifteen homes struck by gunfire; seven homes stoned.

Four schools bombed in the cities of Jacksonville, Nashville, Chattanooga, and Clinton, Tennessee.

Two bombing attempts on schools in Charlotte, North Carolina, and Clinton.

Seven churches bombed, one of which was for whites; attempt made to bomb another Negro church.

One church in Memphis burned, another stoned.

Four Jewish temples or centers burned in Miami, Nashville, Jacksonville, and Atlanta.

Three bombing attempts on Jewish buildings in Charlotte and Gastonia, North Carolina, and Birmingham.

One YWCA building in Chattanooga and an auditorium in Knoxville dynamited.

Two schools burned.

Seventeen towns and cities threatened with mob action.

And there was worse to come.

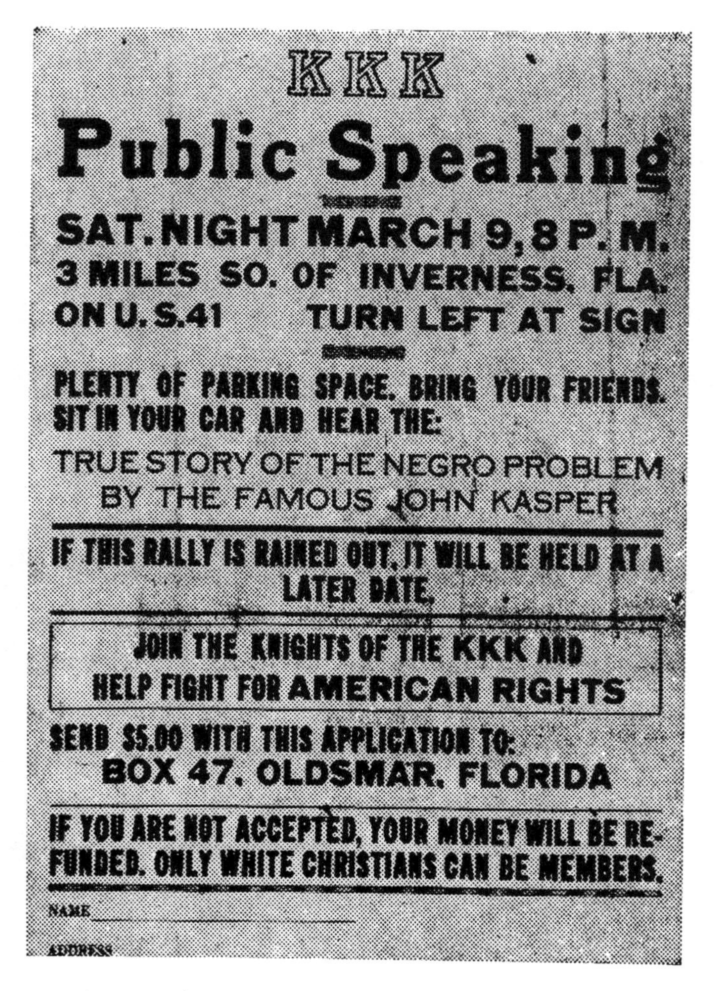

A poster advertising a Klan meeting in Florida in the 1950s.

WIDE WORLD PHOTOS

Klan members burning a cross at a meeting in West Virginia in 1975.

WIDE WORLD PHOTOS

Pro-Klan demonstrators wield bats, nightsticks, and homemade shields as an anti-Klan demonstrator runs from the melee during a rally in Oceanside Calif., in 1980.

AP/WIDE WORLD PHOTOS

Beulah Donald, right,entering the funeral services for her son Michael, slain in Mobile, Ala., in 1981.

UPI/BETTMANN NEWSPHOTOS

After a rally in East Windsor, Conn., in 1986, about two dozen Klansmen and an equal number of onlookers circled a burning cross.

SYGMA

On January 17, 1987, the 58th anniversary of the birth of Martin Luther King, Jr., Klansmen and their backers gathered in Forsyth County, Ga., to shout derogatory comments and throw rocks, bottles and clods of dirt at members of a "Brotherhood March" honoring the slain civil rights leader.

UPI/BETTMANN

In Pulaski, Tenn., the birthplace of the Ku Klux Klan, Klan members marched in protest of a holiday honoring Martin Luther King, Jr., in January, 1988

AP/WIDE WORLD PHOTOS

Pulaski, Tenn., marchers protesting the 1988 holiday honoring Martin Luther King, Jr.

CHAPTER 15

THE CHURCH BOMBING

It was Sunday, September 15, 1963. Sunday school classes had just ended in the Sixteenth Street Baptist Church in Birmingham, Alabama. Mrs. Ella Demand, the Sunday school teacher, had finished reading the lesson for the day—"The Love That Forgives." It was only a few minutes past ten o'clock in the morning when she dismissed her pupils.

Four of them—Denise McNair, Cynthia Wesley, Carol Robertson, and Addie Mae Collins—met in the hallway, then skipped lightly down the stairs to a downstairs lounge to don their choir robes. Three of the four were daughters of Birmingham teachers.

As the young girls—Denise was eleven; the others were fourteen—put on their robes and applied lipstick, a passing car slowed down near the north wall of the church and then sped away. Seconds later, a thunderous explosion blasted the church building apart, showering the gathering congregation with stained glass, chunks of plaster and shattered wood, and burying the four young choir girls in a tomb of debris.

Of all the atrocities committed by hate-demented Klansmen over the years, this was the most unforgivable—the ruthless deed that revolted a nation. *Four young black girls who had been attending Sunday school had been blown to pieces when their church was bombed.* And the deed had been done by Klansmen who proclaimed that *they* were *the* 100 percent Americans!

The atrocious church bombing touched off night-long riots in Birmingham. Outraged blacks roamed the streets, hurling rocks at cars displaying Confederate flags. Fires lit up the night. There were scattered bombings. Police patrolled the streets with dogs and shotguns, and five hundred National Guardsmen were sent into the city to restore order.

Birmingham police had been notorious for a "working relationship" that made them virtually partners of the Klan. And so, when morning came, it caused little surprise that two more blacks had become victims: police had shot and killed one black teenager among the rock-throwers and another who had just been riding his bicycle. Two others—one white, one black—had been wounded.

Governor George Wallace, the bombastic segregationist who had stood in the doorway of the University of Alabama to protest integration, was under court order to end the violence touched off by school-desegregation rulings. Making a gesture, he offered a $5,000 reward for the arrest and conviction of those responsible for the church bombing. It came as no surprise that no one in Birmingham rushed forward to collect the money.

The bombing of the Sixteenth Street Baptist Church was Birmingham's greatest disgrace. A bully of a police commissioner, T. Eugene "Bull" Connor, had used tactics so brutal that a wave of disgust had swept the nation. Laws and court rulings meant nothing to Bull Connor. He hated blacks and flaunted his hatred like a badge of honor. For twenty-three years, in a reign of brutality and terror, he had cowed black leaders and kept Birmingham's schools, theaters, parks, playgrounds, restaurants, and even churches completely segregated.

Then Dr. Martin Luther King, Jr., focused his civil rights drive on Birmingham. A charismatic figure, Dr. King had worked seeming miracles through his campaign of nonviolent demonstrations, a mass movement that kept reminding white, middle-class America of the desperate plight of the Negro in the South. When he turned his attention to Birmingham, Dr. King called it "the most segregated city in the United States."

In April, 1963, Dr. King launched his campaign to desegregate Birmingham, using his customary tactics—sit-ins and marches. Bull Connor reacted by arresting over four hundred blacks. Dr. King sent his followers in groups to worship at white churches. Four churches admitted them, but seventeen turned them away.

Tension grew. On May 2, Bull Connor's police arrested five hundred blacks, mostly high school students, and carried them off to jail in school buses. Dr. King held a mass protest meeting. The following day, some 2,500 blacks surged into downtown Birmingham in a protest demonstration. Bull Connor was ready for them.

He met the demonstrators with police dogs and fire hoses. The dogs were trained to rip off clothing with their teeth; the fire hoses, with seven hundred pounds of pressure, smashed demonstrators against the walls of buildings or to the ground. One especially graphic picture was flashed on television screens and carried on the front pages of newspapers around the world. It showed a huge, snarling dog lunging at a frightened black woman. President John F. Kennedy said that the picture made him sick.

Such was the atmosphere in which the church bombing that killed four Sunday school girls took place. The bombing was the fourth within a month, the fiftieth in a period of twenty years—a record that had given Birmingham the name of "Bombingham."

With this bombing history, it might be expected that state detectives and other investigators would have had some idea about the identity of Klansmen familiar with the use of dynamite. Yet nothing had been done. Inaction had been excused on the ground that it hadn't been possible to find enough legal evidence to justify indictments. Progress had been deterred by enforcement officials' recognition of a fact of life in the South: it was almost impossible to get a jury to convict a white man for a crime against blacks.

The Sunday school church bombing was a deed so hideous, however, that even southern law felt something had to be done. Rumors had it that enforcement officials were fairly certain of the bombers' identities. Chief suspect in the case was Robert Chambliss, who was known to local police as "Dynamite Bob." Born in a working-class section that had become all black, Chambliss had such a poor education that he wrote only with the greatest difficulty. He had a long arrest record, including one charge of "flogging while masked," but he had never been convicted of a serious offense. His hatred of blacks was known to be intense.

A few days after the church blast, Chambliss and two other men were arrested for the crime. They were indicted and went to trial. The jury, however, found them guilty of only the lesser offense of illegal possession of dynamite. And even that verdict was reversed on appeal. Birmingham's record of finding white men innocent, no matter what the crime, remained intact.

Years passed, and the black community became convinced that nothing would ever be done, that justice was a myth. Then, in 1970, a vigorous young prosecutor with a conscience, Bill Baxley, was elected attorney general of Alabama. One of Baxley's first acts in office was to reopen the investigation of the church bombing.

Baxley was an aggressive, rough-and-tumble political fighter, with a vocabulary to match that of a George Wallace or a Huey Long. His reopening of the Birmingham church bombing case brought protests from the hate brigade, and he brushed them off in words that even the semiliterate could understand. Typical was his response to a protest by Edward Fields, of the neo-Nazi National States Right Party. On an official letterhead, Baxley wrote, "My response to your letter of February 19, 1976, is—kiss my ass."

Though the new attorney general often had as many as a dozen investigators working on the case, he was frustrated for years. When he tried to find out what information the FBI had in its massive files, he ran into a stone wall. The FBI had sent fifty agents into Birmingham after the church bombing, but it had taken no action and it guarded its files as if the safety of the nation were at stake.

It was not until February, 1980, that a new Justice Department study of the conduct of the FBI revealed the reason for its lack of action in the church bombing case. The study put the blame squarely on the shoulders of FBI Director J. Edgar Hoover. FBI files showed, the Justice Department report said, that the Birmingham office had made "a significant breakthrough" in the case by December, 1964. The Birmingham office reported it had eyewitnesses who could identify Chambliss and three others, and it asked permission to share its information with federal and state prosecutors. Hoover refused.

The all-powerful FBI director, who sometimes gave indications of being racially biased himself, had always aligned himself with the white southern leadership. Congressmen and senators from the South were among his strongest supporters. And so Hoover turned down the Birmingham FBI office's request for action because, he said, he did not think the chances of obtaining a conviction were very good.

The Birmingham FBI office was determined. Five months later, it again asked Hoover to let it share the information it had gathered. Again, he refused. Not only did he refuse, but he put the results of the FBI investigation in the deep freeze, making the information unavailable to anyone.

Thus, when Baxley began his investigation, he got no help. Even after Hoover died in 1972, the old guard in FBI headquarters in Washington continued to withhold the information, just as Hoover would have done. It was not until 1976 that Baxley was able to break through the wall of FBI super-secrecy and get the information that should have been made available twelve years earlier.

Baxley's motivations have been best described by Patsy Sims in her book, *The Klan*. He was in many ways a typical southerner—but a representative of a new, younger breed of southerner. He liked country music, attended church regularly, and was a great fan of the Alabama football coach, "Bear" Bryant. But when Patsy Sims asked him why he felt more strongly about the Klan than many other southerners who had similar tastes in other respects, Baxley replied:

"'Cause they've gotten away with so much. By the authorities not enforcing the law as far as the Klan's concerned, it has made people in other parts of the country think they are representative of Alabamans or southerners when that's not so. I would like to see that changed. What they do is distasteful to everything America stands for, or should stand for. I just hate 'em."

Despite Baxley's zeal and the help of the FBI's files, his investigation seemed to be going nowhere. The first break came from a twenty-year-old murder that had gone unreported. One of Baxley's investigators picked up a rumor that, in 1957, a twenty-year-old black man had been forced at gunpoint to jump to his death in the Alabama River. His offense? He had been mistaken for another black truck driver who supposedly had committed the "crime" of smiling at a white woman.

The information was so vague that it seemed worthless. But then a suspect being questioned about the church bombing suddenly blurted out, "Man, I got out of the Klan when that guy jumped off the bridge!" Backtracking on this information, detectives finally identified the victim as Willie Edwards, whose body had been found floating in the Alabama River three months after he had been reported missing.

With this information as a lever, Baxley's aides questioned a number of Klan suspects, and one finally broke and confessed. He was Raymond C. Britt, Jr., a jowly mobile-home salesman. He described how he and three associates had picked up Edwards. They had slapped him around a bit, had driven around the countryside most of the night, then had forced him—"crying and sobbing and beggin'" for his life—to jump into the river. Afterward, Britt said, the Klansmen laughed and joked about "that nigger going swimming in the river" in January.

When Britt began to talk, he opened up a whole can of worms. He confessed that he had taken part in four church bombings less than two weeks before the murder of Edwards. He had also fired shots into newly integrated buses. Though he had been arrested, tried, and acquitted for some of these crimes nearly twenty years before, Britt now said, "I wanted to tell the truth after living with this thing for nineteen years."

Baxley became convinced as his detectives dug more deeply into the fatal church bombing that there were two major suspects: "Dynamite Bob" Chambliss, the actual bomber, and, behind him, the man who probably ordered the deed, J. B. Stoner, the neo-Nazi National States Right Party leader from Marietta, Georgia. Even Baxley admitted, however, that it might be difficult to prove a case against Stoner because he was hidden so far back in the shadows, so far removed from the actual deed.

Patsy Sims interviewed Stoner. She wrote: "Once aptly described as resembling a fireplug, he was short and thick, with close-cut curly hair and narrow-slit eyes." He walked with a limp, the result of an early bout with polio. He had lost both parents when quite young, had received only mediocre grades in school, and had become a passionate anti-Semite when he was only sixteen. Sims found him a twisted personality, consumed by hatred for blacks and Jews.

Asked if he advocated violence, Stoner laughed, "Well, I don't advocate it, but if somebody else does it, I never criticize 'em."

"But do you condone it?"

"Niggers are killing white people from one end of the country to the other ever' day, so if a white man kills a nigger, why I say more power to him!"

Earlier, Stoner had been questioned by the House Un-American Activities Committee about his possible involvement in the Birmingham church bombing. Donald Appell, a HUAC investigator, also attempted to question him about two explosions two days later that, Appell said, were intended "to injure FBI agents and other law enforcement personnel in retaliation for their vigorous investigation of the church bombing, including the questioning of many Klan suspects." Stoner had refused to answer any such questions, falling back on his constitutional rights under the Fifth Amendment, which protects a witness from possible self-incrimination. Appell then contended HUAC had information that placed Stoner in Birmingham "immediately prior to, and including, September 15, 1963," the date of the church bombing.

Such was the state of affairs when, in September, 1977, Attorney General Baxley convinced a grand jury to indict both Stoner and Chambliss for the Birmingham bombings. Stoner* fought extradition from Georgia, and so Chambliss alone went to trial.

The most damaging evidence came from Chambliss's own niece by marriage, Elizabeth Cobb, an ordained Methodist minister. She testified that her uncle had told her the day before the church bombing that "he had enough stuff put away to flatten half of Birmingham." She said he was in "a very angry and agitated state" over the recent integration of Birmingham schools. When she urged him not to do anything violent, "he looked me in the face and said, 'You just wait until after Sunday morning and they will beg us to let them segregate.'" Six days later, she testified, she found him watching a television documentary about the church bombing and heard him say, "It wasn't meant to hurt anybody. It didn't go off when it was supposed to."

---

*J. B. Stoner was eventually brought back to Alabama, where he was tried and convicted for his role in the church bombing. While awaiting sentence, he fled, sacrificing his $20,000 bond. He was a fugitive for five months. In June, 1983, he was sentenced to ten years in prison, but served only some three years before he was paroled. He immediately resumed his hate-mongering and was one of the Klan leaders who directed the Forsyth County riots in 1987.

Fortunately, there had been important changes in the South by the late 1970s. Racial hatred had not been wiped out; it still existed under the surface. But restaurants, theaters, and schools had been desegregated. And Chris McNair, the father of the dead Denise, was one of a dozen blacks who had been elected to the Alabama House of Representatives. Even the jury that tried Chambliss had three blacks on it, a kind of integration that would have shocked Alabama two decades previously.

In his summation to the jury, Attorney General Baxley appealed to the better instincts of southerners:

"You've got a chance to do something," he told the jurors, holding up photographs of the four maimed young bodies and the shattered church. "Let the world know that this is not the way the people of Alabama felt then or feel now. It's not going to bring these little girls back, but it will show the world that this murder case has been solved by the people of Alabama. Give Denise a birthday present."

And so, on what would have been Denise McNair's twenty-sixth birthday, the jury returned its verdict. As Chambliss stood to face the jurors, the foreman pronounced one word: "Guilty."

CHAPTER

16

THE LONG HOT SUMMER

THE year 1964 would go down as one of the worst in American history—the year of the long hot summer. It was a year when the U.S. military machine was being geared up for the ultimate folly and tragedy of war in Vietnam, a year when, by contrast, idealistic civil rights workers invaded the South, determined to end the terrorism that had deprived blacks of their rights and kept them from the polls. And so it was a year of confrontation—one in which the Klan struck back in one of its most sadistic outbursts, one in which the full power of the federal government was turned loose to track down the so-called White Knights of Mississippi.

Mississippi became the focus of this miniature civil war for two primary reasons: blacks were being literally starved to death on its plantations, and the white ruling class had so terrorized the black community that only 24,000 blacks were registered to vote out of 400,000 of voting age.

This system had sent to Congress two powerful senators who were like relics of pre–Civil War days. Senator James O. Eastland, whose

5,800-acre plantation in Sunflower County was supported partly by federal farm subsidies while black children starved in shanties all around him, headed the powerful Senate Judiciary Committee. Senator John Stennis, whose native Kemper County had become known as "bloody Kemper" because of the manner in which blacks were murdered or just mysteriously disappeared, had become a power on the Senate Military Affairs Committee and a leading war hawk on Vietnam.

All around these two scions of the Old South, federal officials estimated there were between 60,000 and 100,000 unemployed blacks. Postwar mechanization and chemical weed killers had made black farmhands just so much useless human surplus on the rich, dark soil of the Mississippi Delta. They lived in cardboard-walled shanties, their children huddled together, listless, their bellies distended from malnutrition. The scenes in those cabins reminded reporters and visiting congressmen of the worst pictures they had seen of famine-stricken black Africans.

The inhuman contrasts in this divided society made Mississippi a potential tinderbox. New federal equal rights and voting laws meant nothing to Mississippians—and obviously would continue to mean nothing unless black voters could be registered and obtain power through the ballot box. This could be accomplished only if the terrorized blacks of Mississippi received help. And so in the spring of 1964, the Council of Federated Organizations, a confederation of civil rights groups, decided to send hundreds of young volunteers into Mississippi in late June in a campaign to register those thousands of disenfranchised blacks.

Newspaper accounts of this impending "massive assault" stirred up white animosity in Mississippi unlike anything since the Reconstruction era. Even educated and normally moderate Mississippians recalled the horrors of the Scalawag-Carpetbagger regime that had ruled the state in that post–Civil War period. To them, this influx of northern civil rights workers, backed by the authority of the federal government, seemed like a threatening replay of the hated Reconstruction episode.

In this atmosphere, the Klan revived like some lush, noisome weed popping out of the rich delta soil. It was an almost overnight development. Prior to 1964, there had been relatively little Klan activity in the state. Even in the frenzied period of the 1920s, Mississippi had been the one state in the South in which the Klan had failed. The ruling aristocratic plantation class had blocked it. In subsequent years, the state had relied on its white citizens' councils and its white-controlled state government to keep the blacks in their place. Klan activity and brutality existed, but Klan membership was small and politically ineffective.

The embers of racial animosity remained smoldering, however, and it took only the threat of the civil rights invasion of 1964 to fan those embers into a roaring flame. A Klan group known as the White Knights of Mississippi was formed. It was to become, according to federal investigators later, the most vicious and violent in history—a ruthless band suspected of almost three hundred acts of terrorism.

The power in the White Knights was a man named Sam Holloway Bowers, Jr. He was tall, sandy-haired, a bachelor and a loner. By all accounts, he was a man of superior intelligence, a voracious reader and a talented writer. He was many cuts above the poorly educated, almost illiterate rednecks who usually formed the backbone of the Klan.

Bowers was born in New Orleans in 1924. He was the grandson of a distinguished Mississippi attorney who had served four terms in Congress. Bowers's parents were divorced when he was fourteen, and he had followed his father around the country wherever the latter's sales jobs took him. During World War II, Bowers served in the navy until 1945 when he was discharged as a machinist first class.

After the war, he took college courses in engineering, then returned to Laurel, Mississippi, where he set up a vending-machine business known as the Sambo Amusement Company. He and his partner used living quarters behind the business front of the building.

Bowers never socialized. He had never been known to date. Acquaintances described him as fanatically fond of guns and explosives. They told reporters that he wore a swastika armband, clicked his heels in front of his dog, and saluted, "Heil, Hitler."

He was a man, in other words, intelligent enough and psychologically twisted enough to be extremely dangerous. On the platform, one FBI agent later testified, he was so persuasive that "he can get these people to do near anything." Bowers, indeed, proved the truth of that observation.

On Sunday morning, June 7, 1964, Bowers assembled his legions. The White Knights traveled by dirt roads, coming from all directions to gather at an abandoned church near the town of Raleigh, forty miles southeast of the capital city of Jackson. They all came armed. Guards with shotguns and .45s on their hips checked the arrivals to make certain they belonged to the White Knights. Six men on horseback patrolled the nearby woods. Two small planes circled overhead, maintaining contact with walkie-talkies. Security was iron-tight.

By midmorning, some three hundred White Knights had gathered. Then Bowers rose and delivered a prepared speech, a copy of which was later obtained by the House Un-American Activities Committee.

"Fellow Klansmen," Bowers began, "we are here to discuss what we are going to do about COFO's nigger-Communist invasion of Mississippi which will begin within a few days."

Bowers advised his followers to avoid open, daylight street warfare with the "hordes" of blacks he expected to demonstrate. They should cooperate with the local police as "legally deputized men" in controlling such outbursts. They should, however, have "a secondary group" behind the front lines in the streets. "It must be understood," he said, "that the secondary group is an extremely swift and extremely violent hit-and-run group."

He added, "Any personal attacks on the enemy should be carefully planned to include only the leaders and the prime white collaborators of the enemy forces. These attacks against these selected, individual targets should, of course, be as severe as circumstances and conditions will permit."

Don Whitehead, who described this scene in his book, *Attack on Terror*, later wrote that, by the time the White Knights filed out of the church, they were "committed to a campaign of terror that was to leave a tragic trail of death and destruction, bring shame to Mississippi, challenge the Federal government's enforcement of the civil rights law, and plunge the Federal Bureau of Investigation into a four-year underground fight against Klansmen the like of which the South had never seen."

There had been many warnings of rising Klan activity in Mississippi before Bowers's June rally at the isolated church. In one county, three black homes and a barbershop were firebombed; three reporters and two blacks were beaten. In another county, two civil rights workers were pursued and shot at; four blacks were whipped. Another black was seriously wounded by shotgun fire, and still another was killed. Black churches were damaged or destroyed, black homes bombed or shot at. Crosses blazed across the state. Thousands of posters listing twenty reasons for joining the White Knights were displayed everywhere. One was even tacked to the bulletin board not far from the sheriff's office in the Neshoba County Courthouse in Philadelphia. It remained undisturbed.

This carnival of intensifying violence alarmed federal officials in Washington. Attorney General Robert F. Kennedy sent John Doar, the tall, large-boned, rugged-faced expert in his Civil Rights Division, into Mississippi with a squad of his own civil rights investigators. The attorney general was unhappy with the performance of the FBI, whose local agents were all too often on a buddy basis with sheriffs and policemen who were themselves either members of the Klan or Klan sympathizers.

The fuse was set; only the lighted match was needed to cause an explosion. The White Knights lighted the match on the evening of June 16, 1964, when three blacks were beaten after a meeting at the Mount Zion Church in Longdale. Later that same night, the church was burned.

The assaults and the church-burning drew the attention of three young civil rights workers headquartered in Meridian. They were Michael Schwerner, James Chaney, and Andrew Goodman. Schwerner and Chaney had talked previously to the black leaders of the Mount Zion Church, and so they felt a personal interest in what had happened. On Sunday, June 21, they and Goodman drove from Meridian to Longdale to talk to their black friends.

On their way back, they were stopped by Deputy Sheriff Cecil Price. He accused Chaney, who was driving Schwerner's station wagon, of speeding. He held Schwerner and Goodman "for investigation."

Price took his prisoners to the Neshoba County Courthouse in Philadelphia, Mississippi. His superior, Sheriff Lawrence E. Rainey, was on hand at the time, though it could never be established what role, if any, he played in the events that followed. All that is known is that the three prisoners were shoved into cells and held for about four hours, presumably to allow enough time for a squad of White Knights executioners to be assembled. Then, about 10:30 P.M., the three were released by Price and told to get out of town.

They got back into Schwerner's station wagon and headed out of Philadelphia. Deputy Sheriff Price in an official car and two other cars loaded with Klansmen followed them. About sixteen miles south of Philadelphia, the fugitives were stopped again by Price. This time, they were driven back up the road and then down a sandy track leading into deep woods. That was the last that was heard of them.

When the three young men did not return to Meridian, their fellow civil rights workers became alarmed. They began calling local, state, and federal officials. A missing persons alarm was sent out. Attorney General Kennedy, having little faith, from past experience, in the diligence of local and state officials, ordered the FBI to treat the case as a kidnapping. Kidnapping is a federal offense.

FBI Director Hoover, so pressured, sent Inspector Joseph Sullivan, one of the bureau's best troubleshooters, to Meridian with a squad of five agents. On the same day, June 23, Schwerner's burned-out station wagon was discovered in an isolated, wooded area. The charred remains of the car banished any doubt that Schwerner, Goodman, and Chaney had been killed. Outrage swept the nation.

President Lyndon B. Johnson was one of those most outraged. In no uncertain terms, he ordered reluctant FBI Director Hoover to get down to Meridian himself and to throw the full resources of the bureau into the hunt for the murderers. Having no choice, Hoover went. Even then, he made it clear that he personally was friendly with the governor and the local politicians, but he announced that, in response to the President's order, he was bringing 153 more FBI agents into Mississippi.

The newly arrived agents were not hampered by longtime, close personal ties with local policemen, and they threw themselves into their task with zeal. They were confronted at the outset with a knotty problem. No one doubted that the civil rights workers had been murdered, but no trace of them had been found. Without corpses, murder remained only a suspicion, not a crime that could be prosecuted.

A small army of searchers fanned out throughout the muggy pinelands and swamps, hunting the missing trio. FBI agents, servicemen from the nearby Kessler Air Force Base, state highway patrolmen, and even deputies from the game and fish commission all joined in the manhunt. It went on for days and days, and then for weeks. Still there was no trace of the missing men. It began to seem as if they would never be found.

All the time this hunt was being pressed, however, the new FBI team was hard at work. Among the agents was an elite squad known as the "Big Ten." They were called that because they were physically large and strong and because, it was sometimes said, they did not mind bending the law a bit in pressuring Klansmen to give them the information they wanted. This tough questioning was only one string to the FBI's bow; the other was money. Tempting sums were offered to members of the White Knights to persuade them to become informers.

The money did the trick. Even the fanatic White Knights were not immune to its temptation. On August 2, 1964, an informant came up with the information the FBI had to have, and the bodies of the three young civil rights workers were discovered in a large earthen dam where they had been entombed. The bodies were so badly decomposed that the fingers had to be severed and sent to FBI fingerprint headquarters in Washington for identification.

With the grisly evidence he needed, John Doar moved swiftly. Twenty-one men, six identified by the FBI as White Knights, were arrested. Included among the suspects were Sheriff Rainey and his deputy, Cecil Price. Now began a long court battle.

Federal authorities were limited in what they could do. Murder is not a federal offense; murder must be tried in local courts under state laws. And Mississippi officials refused to recognize that murder had been committed. They did not contend that the three young men had shot themselves and then buried themselves in the dam. They simply ignored the whole business.

This left rugged John Doar with only one alternative. The White Knights, in kidnapping the trio, had not taken them across state lines, and so the only federal charge Doar could bring against the murderers was a relatively minor one: conspiracy to deprive Schwerner, Goodman, and Chaney of their civil rights. Three years of legal wrangling ensued. Southern judges, as blindly prejudiced as the politicians, threw out the indictments in an effort to erect a protective shield around the Klansmen. It was not until February, 1967, that Doar got a grand jury to reinstate the indictments so that the accused could be brought to trial in federal court.

Eighteen defendants were left when the trial began in October. The major figures were Sheriff Rainey, Deputy Sheriff Price, and Sam Bowers. Doar charged that Bowers had plotted the crime. His case was based largely on the testimony of paid informers. The Reverend Delmar Dennis, who had been a top aide to Bowers, had been paid $15,000 by the FBI. He identified nine of the defendants as members of the White Knights, and he testified about a meeting of the Klavern at which it had been announced that Bowers had ordered the "elimination" of Schwerner.

Other White Knights, turned witnesses, filled out the story. One was a Meridian policeman, Sgt. Miller, who had received $3,400 in salary and travel expenses after he became an FBI informer in September, 1964. Even one of the defendants, James E. Jordan, turned state's evidence and described how the three victims had been deliberately detained in the Neshoba County jail to give the Klan time to get together its execution squad.

Jordan testified that he had been stationed as a lookout on the lonely road that had been selected as the murder site. "I heard doors slam, some loud talk that I could not distinguish, and then I heard several shots," he testified. When he walked down the road a few minutes later, he said, he saw the three bodies sprawled on the ground.

Another defendant, Horace Doyle Barnette, backed up Jordan's account—but with one important difference. According to Barnette, just after Schwerner and Goodman had been shot, Jordan came running to the scene, yelling, "Save one for me." Then, seeing Chaney, "Jordon stood in the middle of the road and shot him," Barnette said.

He added that Jordan had complained, "You didn't leave me anything but a nigger."

In his summation to the jury, John Doar recognized the natural prejudice against informers and dealt with it eloquently. He said, "Much has been and will be said about the extraordinary methods used in discovering the guilty. Should it have been otherwise? Was this a case to be forgotten? Was this not a case for the maximum effort of the FBI? Could the Federal Government have succeeded in any...way other than rewards, payment for information tending to expose the band of murderous conspirators, the midnight killers, to bring them to the bar of justice...?"

The jurors heeded the argument and convicted Deputy Sheriff Price, Sam Bowers, and five others. The rest, including Sheriff Rainey, against whom Doar admitted there was no direct evidence, were acquitted. Bowers and one of the other defendants were sentenced to ten years in prison; the remaining five drew terms of from three to six years. By July, 1976, with time off for good behavior, most of them were out of prison and living in the Meridian-Philadelphia area. Sheriff Rainey, though acquitted, had been stripped of his badge and moved from job to job as a security guard.

As for murder, the state of Mississippi still did not recognize that it had been committed. It never filed murder charges against any of the defendants.

CHAPTER

17

MISSISSIPPI was not the only southern state to be disgraced by the violence and depravity that marked the long hot summer of 1964. Flames of racial hatred roared through the South, and the killings mounted, each seeming more outrageous than the last.

Lieutenant Colonel Lemuel A. Penn had fought in the Pacific during World War II. After the war, he had remained in the Army Reserve. In civilian life, he was the director of vocational and adult education in Washington, D.C.

In the summer of 1964, he spent two weeks on active-duty training at Fort Benning, Georgia. His tour ended July 10, and a few minutes after midnight, early on July 11, he started to drive back to his home in Washington. With him were two other black officers, Lieutenant Colonel John D. Howard and Major Charles E. Brown, both of whom also worked in the Washington school system.

The men were traveling in Brown's white Chevrolet, and Brown drove the first leg of the trip. At Athens, Georgia, around 4:00 A.M., they stopped to change drivers, and Penn took the wheel.

Brown went to sleep in the front seat, and Howard was lying down in the back, as Penn headed northeast on Highway 72. At Colbert, he swung north on 172. About twelve miles out of town, he drove onto a bridge over the Broad River. As he did, a car traveling at high speed came up from behind, turned out to pass, and two shotgun blasts split the night. One charge of heavy shot ripped into Colonel Penn's left jaw, killing him instantly.

Brown and Howard escaped injury only because they had been slumped down. They managed to get the wildly careening car under control as the one carrying the shotgun-assassins sped away. It was just 4:50 A.M.

Here was an atrocity that sent another shock wave rippling across the nation. Colonel Penn had fought for his country in World War II. He was still an officer, returning home after putting in his two-week training stint at Fort Benning. And he had not been safe on the highways of the nation he had fought to defend.

FBI Director Hoover rushed an assistant director and twenty FBI agents into Athens to back up the small number of local agents on the scene. The agents concentrated at once on the names of known Klansmen, checking their whereabouts during the early-morning hours of July 11.

The Georgia Klansmen were members of another splinter group headed by Robert Shelton, who called himself the Imperial Wizard of the United Klans of America. Shelton insisted that his UKA support had been instrumental in electing George Wallace governor of Alabama, but his entire national membership totaled something less than 20,000. Like the White Knights of Mississippi, however, Shelton's rednecks were a vicious gang of thugs.

FBI agents had no clues when they started to investigate Colonel Penn's murder. They put in three intensive weeks of almost around-the-clock surveillance and interrogation. At the end of that time, they had their suspects. They were Howard Sims, Cecil Myers, and James

Lackey, all members of the Clark County Klavern 244 of Shelton's United Klans of America.

Lackey cracked. He finally confessed that he was driving the assassins' car when the shotgun blasts were fired. He said, "We thought some out-of-town niggers might stir up some trouble in Athens. We had intended scaring off out-of-town colored people before they could give us any trouble. When the Washington, D.C., car was spotted...we thought they might be out-of-towners and might cause trouble. Sims and Myers kept insisting that I follow the car...They had me go out of town so it wouldn't seem like someone from Athens did the shooting. I had no idea that they would really shoot the niggers and was very surprised when two shots were fired. Sims fired one shot, and Myers fired one shot..."

Sims and Myers were brought to trial on murder charges in Georgia's circuit court. It was the same old story. Southern juries refused to convict southern white men for killing blacks, even though in this case the victim had been a military officer. Both Sims and Myers were acquitted.

The federal government, just as it had had to do in Mississippi, then took over in an attempt to see that some kind of justice was done. Sims and Myers were brought to trial in federal court in 1966 on the charge of conspiring to deny black citizens their constitutional rights. This time, both were convicted and given ten-year prison sentences. The U.S. Supreme Court refused to overturn the verdict, and so both Sims and Myers ultimately went to prison.

Before they did, another outrage, this time in Alabama, provoked a national uproar. Again, this was the work of Robert Shelton's United Klans, but this time the solution was swift and sure. The rapid solution at the time resulted from the fact that the FBI had an informant highly placed in the ranks of Shelton's United Klans of America.

This man was Gary Thomas Rowe, a six-foot-two-inch redhead

weighing 220 pounds, all of it muscle. Had Rowe ever trained as a prizefighter, he might have created a stir in the heavyweight division because he certainly had a knockout punch. The late William P. Sullivan, who was in charge of intelligence for Hoover and became the FBI's No. 2 man in Washington before he split with the director, later related this story, illustrating Rowe's awesome physical prowess:

Rowe stopped at an Alabama roadstand late one night and ordered a cup of coffee. Before he could be served, four members of a Hell's Angels–type motorcycle gang stalked in. One of the young toughs told Rowe he would have to wait until they had been served. That was his big mistake. Sullivan wrote, "Rowe hauled off and belted him, knocking him silly. With that, the rest of them jumped on Rowe, and when it was over three of the men went to the hospital. The fourth ran off and left his motorcycle."

Such a man was the informer who had swaggered and bullied his way through the UKA until Shelton trusted him completely. Many UKA members had become suspicious of Rowe, according to his own account, because there were just too many leaks to the FBI coming out of the supposedly supersecret Klan councils. But Rowe, with his powerful fists and brazen gall, always outfaced the grumbling doubters and convinced them that he was the most loyal of the loyal.

This was the situation when on March 25, 1965, Rowe received orders from his Klan superiors to join three others on a day-long surveillance in Montgomery, Alabama's capital city. He notified his FBI control officer, Neil Shanahan, and Shanahan told him, "Go."

So it came about that Rowe found himself sitting in a red and white Chevrolet with three other Klansmen—Gene Thomas, William Orville Eaton, and Collie Leroy Wilkins. They drove to Montgomery, where some twelve thousand demonstrators were massed around the Capitol.

The Montgomery demonstration was the climax of Dr. Martin Luther King, Jr.'s historic march from Selma to Montgomery to dramatize the plight of poor southern blacks. Civil rights workers from the North had joined the march. One of these was Mrs. Viola Liuzzo, a Detroit housewife and the mother of five children.

A civil rights activist, Mrs. Liuzzo used her car to carry some of the marchers back to Selma after the demonstration in front of the Capitol broke up. After delivering her passengers, she started back toward Montgomery on Highway 80. Sitting beside her was a black youth, Leroy Motion, age nineteen.

According to the story Rowe later told on the witness stand and in his book, *My Undercover Years With the Ku Klux Klan*, Mrs. Liuzzo's car drew alongside theirs at a red light. The sight of the black youth sitting beside the blonde mother in her thirties was enough to set the juices of racial hate flowing.

"I'll be damned," Rowe quoted Wilkins as saying. "We've finally caught two of the bastards together. Let's take 'em."

Rowe said he was sitting in the back seat of the car, behind the driver. Wilkins was sitting on the right side of the front seat, Eaton in the right rear seat, as the chase began down the highway. Gene Thomas, the driver, speeded up to pass. Rowe later wrote: "Just as Wilkins's arm was almost even with the front window of the woman's automobile, she turned her head and looked at us. I guess the only thing she could see was the muzzle of his gun—the most awful expression came over her face that God knows I have ever seen in my life—and in that instant Wilkins fired two shots at her head... Then all I could see was glass cracking and splintering, and all I could hear was gunfire. As we passed the car, Wilkins and Eaton emptied their guns at the windshield."

A .38 caliber slug had torn into Mrs. Liuzzo's left temple, killing her instantly. Her car, out of control, plunged off the road into a field where young Motion managed to turn off the ignition and escape.

The killers stopped their car a short distance down the road, and Wilkins ran back to make certain there were no witnesses around.

Finding no one, he came back, flipped the discharged cartridges onto the roof of the car, and reloaded his gun.

As soon as Rowe could shake his companion, he telephoned Neil Shanahan, who confirmed his worst fears. Mrs. Liuzzo was dead.

"You know who did it, Tom?" Shanahan asked.

"I was in the automobile. Wilkins killed her," Rowe told him.

Shanahan instructed Rowe to meet him in the parking lot of the West End Baptist Hospital in Birmingham. There, Rowe handed the FBI agent his revolver, a Smith and Wesson with a two-inch barrel. "Smell it; check it; make sure it hasn't been fired," he told Shanahan.

Rowe later led FBI agents to the spot where he said Wilkins had flipped out his spent cartridges. Five casings were found that the FBI laboratory identified as having been fired from the .38 caliber revolver owned by Gene Thomas. According to Rowe, Wilkins used Thomas's revolver because Thomas was driving the car.

With the undercover man as their ace in the hole, FBI agents rounded up the other Klansmen before noon on the day after the murder. The arrests touched off another long round of court cases. A federal jury convicted Thomas, Eaton, and Wilkins of conspiring to deprive Mrs. Liuzzo of her civil rights. They were sentenced to ten-year prison terms.

State prosecutors tried twice to convict the Klansmen of murder. Eaton had died, and so only Thomas and Wilkins went on trial on the murder charges. Rowe later wrote that, at the first trial, two of the jurors were White Citizens' Council members. He protested to the prosecutors handling the case. He said that these men had the same ideas as the Klan and urged that they be removed. The prosecutor didn't listen—and wound up with a hung jury, the two holdouts being the White Citizens' Council members of whom Rowe had been suspicious.

A second trial in October, 1965, turned out even worse. Thomas and

Wilkins were found not guilty, a verdict that seemed to say it was still difficult, if not impossible, to get southern juries to convict killers in racially motivated cases.

Even this was not the end of the story. In 1978, after serving their prison terms, Thomas and Wilkins charged that Rowe himself had killed Mrs. Liuzzo. Alabama authorities, who had tried to convict Thomas and Wilkins of the murder, now did an about-face and picked up the cudgels for the two ex-convicts. And a Lowndes County grand jury in September, 1978, indicted Rowe himself for first-degree murder.

It would be hard to imagine a more tangled skein in the sacred halls of justice. The men convicted in federal court, once out of prison, turn accusers and get the state to indict for the same crime the very witness who put them behind bars!

This was too much. A Federal District Court judge in Montgomery quashed the Lowndes County indictment. He ruled that, since Rowe had been given immunity for his testimony against Thomas and Wilkins, the state courts could not touch him.

CHAPTER

18

A KLAN UNDONE

ROBERT Shelton's United Klans of America was the largest and most violent of the Klans that rampaged across the South in the 1960s and 1970s. Its members were responsible for the murders of Viola Liuzzo in Alabama and Lemuel Penn in Georgia. Yet, despite federal prosecutions and convictions, the UKA continued to flourish, riding the terror trail until... Until it committed a crime so atrocious it led to its own undoing.

It happened in Mobile, Alabama, on March 21, 1981. Michael Donald was a nineteen-year-old black. He had been watching television in his home until almost midnight, then left to walk to a neighborhood store to buy cigarets. On his way back home, he was stopped by two Klansmen in a car. They waved a gun at him, forced him into the car and sped away.

The next morning young Michael Donald was found hanging from the limb of a camphor tree in a racially mixed neighborhood just a mile from the Mobile police station. He had been savagely beaten with more than a hundred blows, then his throat had been cut—and then, already dead, he had been hanged with a rope knotted thirteen times around his neck. It had not been enough for the Klansmen just to kill; they had wanted to make a public exhibition of their gruesome handiwork.

A group of them gathered on the front porch of a house across the street from the camphor tree. Among them was Bennie Jack Hays, sixty-four, the Titan of Unit 900 of the United Klans. Authorities learned much later from some of the Klansmen that Hays had exulted: "A pretty sight. That's gonna look good on the news. Gonna look good for the Klan."

Hays then walked across the street and stood looking up admiringly at Donald's body—a pose in which television cameras caught him, much to his future distress.

It took two years and two FBI investigations to find out who had killed Michael Donald. But eventually detectives obtained a confession from James (Tiger) Knowles, who was just seventeen at the time of the crime. According to him and other Klansmen, this is what had happened:

A black man accused of murdering a white policeman in Birmingham had been on trial that week in Mobile. The jury, which had some blacks on it, had been unable to reach a verdict. This failure to convict enraged the Klan.

Klansmen who attended Unit 900's weekly meeting quoted Bennie Hays as saying: "If a black man can get away with killing a white man, we ought to be able to get away with killing a black man."

On the Friday night that the trial ended, Klansmen got together in a house that Bennie Hays owned. According to Tiger Knowles's later testimony, he borrowed a pistol, and Henry Francis Hays, Bennie's twenty-six-year-old son, got a length of rope. Then they got into Henry's car and went searching for a black victim.

It was Michael Donald's misfortune that he just happened to be walking on the street that night. Hays and Knowles spotted him, forced him into the car at gunpoint and drove into a neighboring county.

Donald was pleading for his life. When the car stopped, he jumped out and tried to escape. Hays and Knowles pursued, caught him and beat him with a tree limb until he was unconscious. Then they wrapped the rope around his neck; Henry Hays shoved his boot into Donald's face, grabbed the rope and pulled hard. And then they slashed Donald's throat.

They put Donald's body into the trunk of the car and drove back to Bennie Hays's house, where they exhibited their handiwork. The hyped-up Klansmen then burned a cross in front of the Mobile County Courthouse and hung Donald's body from the tree.

It was not until June, 1983, that the FBI obtained the confession that broke the case. Knowles and Henry Hays were arrested for the murder. Both were convicted, Knowles receiving a life sentence, Hays condemned to die.

In most cases, that would have been the end of the story, but not this time. Enter Morris Dees, cofounder of the Southern Poverty Law Center whose KLANWATCH is one of the most authoritative sources on Klan activities. Dees proposed a novel tactic. He suggested that Donald's mother, Beulah Mae Donald, bring a civil suit against the Klan seeking damages for the murder of her son.

Dees contended that the Klan itself, right up to Imperial Wizard Robert Shelton, was as liable as Hays and Knowles because it encouraged such murderous acts. Dees argued that, just as a corporation sets policy and is responsible for acts committed in its name, so Unit 900, the United Klans of America and their top officers were liable for Donald's murder.

Mrs. Donald and her attorney, State Senator Michael A. Figures, agreed to file the civil suit against the Klan and six past and present Klan leaders. Dees and his investigators spent eighteen months getting the evidence for the civil case. In February, 1987, the trial began.

This time Mrs. Donald was among the spectators. She hadn't attended the 1983 trial in which Knowles and Hays were convicted, but now she nerved herself, saying: "If they could stand to kill Michael, I can stand to see their faces."

But she couldn't force herself to look at Tiger Knowles, the first witness. He described in unemotional tones the events that had led up to the killing. Then he stepped down from the witness stand and demonstrated how he had helped to kill Michael Donald.

Other former Klansmen testified that they had been directed by their leaders to harass, intimidate and kill blacks, testimony essential to proving Dees's theory of corporatelike responsibility. The Klan lawyers cross-examined Dees's witnesses, but called none of their own. After four days, testimony ended and the case was ready for final arguments.

At this point, Knowles said that he wished to make a statement. With the judge's permission, he stood in front of the jury and said: "I know that people's tried to discredit my testimony. I've got people after me now. Everything I said is true...I was acting as a Klansman when I done this. And I hope that people learn from my mistake..."

As Knowles finished, he turned to Beulah Mae Donald and begged her forgiveness.

"I can't bring your son back," he said, sobbing. "God knows if I could trade places with him I would."

He vowed to spend the rest of his life trying to make amends.

"I do forgive you," Mrs. Donald told him. "From the day I found out who you all was, I asked God to take care of y'all, and He has."

The all-white jury was out just four hours. Then it did an unprecedented thing: it brought in a $7 million verdict against the Klan.

It was the first time in history that a jury had held the Ku Klux Klan, the organization itself, responsible for the actions of its members. It was a devastating blow to the United Klan, which was stripped of all its possessions, even its own headquarters, a two-story, red brick building set in 6.5 acres of woodland near Lake Tuscaloosa. The building included meeting rooms, dormitories and the private office of Imperial Wizard Robert Shelton. It was turned over to Mrs. Donald and later sold for $55,000.

Mrs. Donald's lawyer, Michael Figures, said they would try to attach the property of Klan leaders. "We don't think we'll get $7 million," he said. "But we think this case marks the last lynching of a black man by the Ku Klux Klan."

It remains to be seen whether that hope is too optimistic, but one thing was certain: the United Klan was suffering further blows. As a result of the testimony in the civil suit, the Mobile district attorney obtained murder indictments against Bennie Jack Hays and his son-in-law, Benjamin F. Cox, twenty-six. The pair went on trial in February, 1988.

Defense attorneys used peremptory challenges to knock sixteen blacks off the trial jury. But then, after the trial started before an all-white jury, Bennie Jack Hays collapsed in the courtroom and had to be taken to a hospital. The judge declared a mistrial and dismissed the jury.

A second trial would have to be held, but the state wanted first to get a ruling to prevent the selection of a racist jury. In a brief it filed, it cited "the increasing amount of white hate group violence against minorities" and stressed that U.S. Justice Department figures for 1986, the latest available, showed that more than 81,000 blacks had been the victims of white crimes, including rape, robbery and assault. In such circumstances, how could justice be obtained from a racially stacked jury?

The state, joined by the Southern Poverty Law Center and other groups, has asked the U.S. Supreme Court to rule on this issue. The court in a previous decision had barred prosecutors from racially stacking juries, but it had not applied the rule to defense counsel. Another trial for Hays and Cox remains in limbo until the issue is settled.

As for Imperial Wizard Robert Shelton, who for more than a quarter of a century ruled the most violent Klan in America, the repeated blows stemming from the Donald case brought him low. In poor health, his membership and revenues depleted, he became a part-time automobile salesman and went into virtual retirement.

CHAPTER 19

THE EXTREMISTS

THE Klan fades away only to be reborn in more violent form.

The $7 million verdict that crippled Robert Shelton's once-powerful UKA, an award that would have been incredible a decade earlier, was just one sign of the passing of the old order. Klansmen who had been responsible for the worst atrocities—the Birmingham church bombing, the murders of Mrs. Liuzzo and Colonel Penn—had been discredited and convicted for their crimes. Klan leadership was in disarray.

But hate and bigotry lived on, fueled to new frenzy by what was perceived as a lost cause in a nation that was turning its back on the old Klans and their message.

The South had become integrated. Black voters were no longer so terrorized that they stayed away from the polls. They voted, and blacks became mayors and council members in Southern towns and sat in state legislatures. Blacks no longer had to give way to whites and move to the back of the bus; they were no longer barred from restaurants, but were welcomed like any other patrons. To Klansmen and their followers, this was like a world turned upside down.

Two national policies, school integration and affirmative action, intensified their grievances. The first stemmed from a 1954 U.S. Supreme Court decision mandating school integration. To achieve this it became necessary to bus students from local to more distant schools to ensure necessary racial mix. Many whites, in both North and South, were outraged.

Affirmative action was the second explosive issue. Blacks and other minority groups were given preference for jobs as an atonement for racial discrimination in the past. Public payrolls were supposed to reflect the racial mixture in a community. Quotas were set requiring the hiring of specific percentages of blacks or members of other minorities. This, the Klan charged, was "reverse discrimination."

Capitalizing on the passions aroused by these issues, Klan leaders at first tried to whip up protests through mass rallies and marches. And some such as Tom Metzger tried to enter the political process. But the realization slowly dawned as the Forsyth Klansman had shouted: "Boys, we've lost this country." Then many Klan leaders in their frustration turned to violence; they began to train with high-powered weapons and to advocate the overthrow of the national government.

One Klan leader who adopted the rabble-rousing but nonrevolutionary tactic was David Duke, who headed the Knights of the Ku Klux Klan. A lanky six feet two, well dressed, smooth talking, Duke was handsome, suave and educated—the antithesis of the stereotypical redneck ruffian.

Yet in his career and conduct he typified a basic problem of the Klan: how to speak the rednecked ruffian's language and how, at the same time, to appear reasonable to larger audiences. It was this conflict between underlying purposes and public posture that bedeviled the militant Skinheads of the 1980s. In television appearances they seemed baffled, unable to explain in reasonable terms their savagely racist policies.

David Duke personified this dilemma. He had joined the Klan at seventeen and had worked his way through Louisiana State University. He had cloaked himself in boyish reasonableness, using words like "gosh" and "golly"—and at the same time he had worn a storm trooper's uniform complete with swastika while picketing William Kunstler, the civil rights attorney. The exhibition had won him the title of "the Nazi of LSU."

Duke was a true Dr. Jekyll and Mr. Hyde of politics and the Klan. In his "respectable' Dr. Jekyll personna he ran for the state senate in Baton Rouge's Sixth Senatorial District in 1975. Appealing to white suburban, middle-class voters, he sugar-coated the Klan's racist message. He was "staunchly" opposed to forced busing; he was against reverse discrimination "going on against white people in employment, promotions and scholarships"; he was against gun control laws and tax increases; he favored stronger criminal laws and free enterprise. Though Duke was soundly defeated, he still polled 33 percent of the vote.

Then, just a year later, the Mr. Hyde part of his personality was on display in New Orleans, where police arrested him for inciting to riot. The police accused him of leading a Klan mob that surrounded a police car, pounding, beating and shaking it. The officers trapped in the car later testified that they had feared for their lives. Other witnesses declared that Duke had urged his followers on by calling the policemen "commie Jews." Duke ridiculed the charges, but in August, 1979, he was found guilty in a Louisiana court.

Duke reacted with vituperation. Speaking at a mass rally in Texas, in an auditorium resounding with screams of "White power! White power!" he dropped the mask of respectability and words like "nigger" came pouring from his lips. He attacked reverse discrimination, black welfare, oppression of the white race, and Jewish control of the media. "I say if the Jews can have their state in Israel, we can have our state right here in the United States!" he thundered. "We have a right as the white majority to run this country as we see fit!" He denounced the policemen in New Orleans as "pimps" and said perhaps he should have incited a riot.

Despite such exhibitions, the other David Duke—the handsome, spuriously engaging personality—became something of a television star, appearing on talk shows across the country. This reception encouraged him to turn more to politics. He established his own National Party and ran for President of the United States in 1980, 1984 and 1988, polling in each instance only a handful of votes.

Then, in February, 1989, Duke shocked the leadership of the Republican Party by winning a seat in the lower house of the Louisiana legislature. Running in Metairie, a white bedroom suburb of New Orleans, he posed as the founder and leader of the National Association for the Advancement of White People. He claimed he was no longer affiliated with the Klan, but a phone listing for the Klan was the same as his home number. President George Bush and former President Ronald Reagan, worried that a Duke victory might label their party racist, pleaded with voters to vote for Duke's opponent, John Treen. But the voters of Metairie did not listen.

A principal lieutenant of David Duke spurned this working-within-the-system approach and opted for violence. Louis Beam, the Texas Grand Titan, boasted at the national convention of Duke's Klan that his Texas unit had "a military program." Then he shouted: "We are getting ready to reclaim Texas for the white man...so get ready...Get ready for what we know is coming. Everyone talks of a race war. How many guns, bullets, food, training, preparations have you made? Our forefathers built this country with courage and blood. It will take fresh blood, but, by God, a lot of it will be the blood of our enemies...The government is murdering our people, busing our children, supporting communist governments. There are penalties for murder: death. And they are guilty of murder! Prepare for what is coming!"

How did the "respectable" David Duke react to this ranting speech?

He promoted Louis Beam from Grand Titan to Grand Dragon of the Lone Star State.

Beam, a workaholic, soon built the Texas Knights into the strongest unit in the KKK. He established a paramilitary arm and named it the Texas Emergency Reserve (TER). It was composed of ex-servicemen and some active-duty personnel, and it conducted military training at several sites in east Texas.

In 1981 Beam and the TER conducted an often violent campaign against Vietnamese fishermen in the Galveston area. Local prejudices were whipped up against the Vietnamese for taking away the livelihood of American fishermen. Boats were sabotaged and sometimes burned. This campaign of racial intimidation was finally brought to a halt by a suit filed by the Southern Poverty Center's KLANWATCH against Beam and the Klan. A federal judge ordered the harassment to stop and banned paramilitary activity.

Beam's reaction was to plunge more deeply into the world of violence. In late 1981 he turned up at Hayden Lake, Idaho, at the home of the Aryan Nations. Here he wrote *Essays of a Klansman,* a series highlighted by an assassination point system for racists wanting to attain the status of "Aryan Warrior." Point values were established for various types of assassinations, ranging from "street niggers" to the President of the United States. Killing a street cop counted for one-tenth of a point; the killing of the president, a full point. Earning enough credits to total one point made one an "Aryan Warrior."

This assassination point system was adopted by the Order, the most violent of the Klan splinter groups dedicated to waging guerrilla warfare. Beam had close ties to The Order (some asserted he was a member) and was known by the code names Nathan Bedford Forrest, Turner Ashby and "Lone Star." He was a leading advocate of what Klansmen called the "Fifth Era" strategy, a movement designed to take the Klan out of the public eye and to make it an underground, terrorist group.

The Order grew out of this strategy. It was founded in the Pacific Northwest in 1983 by Robert Matthews and was an offshoot of the Aryan Nations of Hayden Lake. Matthews gathered twenty-three fanatics around him and set out to make war on the government. Of the twenty-three Order members, five had known ties to the Klan, six to the Aryan Nations, four to another warlike group known as The Covenant, The Sword and The Arm of the Lord.

Money was needed to finance Matthews's envisioned revolution, and The Order adopted two tactics to get it: a counterfeiting operation was set up at Hayden Lake, and Matthews led his followers on a bank-robbing spree in the Northwest.

In March, 1984, four men led by Matthews stole more than $40,000 from an armored car in Seattle, Washington. On April 23 a six-man squad held up a parked Continental Armored Car transport truck and escaped with $500,000 in cash.

Racist acts kept step with the holdups. A Seattle porno theater was bombed; a Boise, Idaho, synagogue was set on fire. And on June 18, 1984, Alan Berg, a Denver talk-show host, was assassinated. Berg, a Jew, had infuriated The Order by his denunciations of racist extremists. A four-man hit squad was organized; they caught Berg in the driveway of his home and riddled him with bullets.

The most sensational holdup of The Order's crime spree followed a month later. On July 19 a dozen men forced a Brink's truck off the road near Ukiah, California. They shot out the truck's tires and sprayed it with automatic weapons fire. Then they blocked the highway and diverted and rerouted traffic while they made off with $3.6 million in cash.

The string of bank and armored car holdups brought the Federal Bureau of Investigation into the case. In December, 1984, the FBI caught up with Matthews, The Order's founder. One hundred heavily armed agents trapped him in a house on remote Whitbey Island near Seattle; in the gunfight that followed, Matthews was killed.

His followers were soon indicted in federal court. According to affidavits the FBI obtained from Order members and testimony at the subsequent trial, the proceeds of The Order's multi-million-dollar crime spree had been used to purchase large tracts of land in Idaho and Missouri where recruits were to have been trained in paramilitary activities. The money was also used to purchase vehicles and a small arsenal of weapons and explosives. And some of that last $3.6 million haul was spread around to leaders in the underground movement. Louis Beam reportedly received $100,000 and Tom Metzger between $260,000 and $300,000.

Beam's activities especially drew investigators' attention. He had set up a cross-country computer network linking racist leaders. According to affidavits obtained by the FBI, he had discussed long-range plans to sabotage railroads and utilities and sewer systems, to assassinate federal judges, and to train recruits in guerrilla warfare. Beam was called the ambassador at large for the Aryan Nations, and he was allied with the militant The Covenant, The Sword and The Arm of the Lord.

The CSA had a 224-acre compound in a remote wooded area on Ball Shoals Lake on the Arkansas-Missouri border. FBI agents, aided by other law enforcement officials, lay siege to the camp on April 19, 1985. After a three-day standoff, they captured it—and were amazed at what they found: a weapons cache sufficient for a small army that included an antitank rocket launcher with missile; grenades, land mines and antiaircraft guns; seventy-seven semiautomatic and automatic weapons; fifty sticks of dynamite; two-and-a-half pounds of C-4 explosives; and a truck chassis being converted into an armored car.

Indictments followed, accusing the CSA of seditious conspiracy. One of those indicted was Louis Beam. Though he had never been convicted of any crime, he became a fugitive and for five months was on the FBI's Ten Most Wanted list. He was finally arrested by Mexican police on November 6, 1987, and was brought back to the United States to stand trial.

The trial was held in Fort Smith, Arkansas. Thirteen CSA members had been indicted; of these, seven had already been convicted of other crimes, but they were included in the seditious conspiracy case. An all-white jury on April 7, 1988, acquitted Beam and the other twelve. The acquittal apparently resulted from the jury's acceptance of the defense contention that Beam and the other twelve had been merely exercising their right of free speech when they advocated assassinations.

An entirely different verdict was rendered in The Order trial in Seattle. Here there was no question that talk and actual crimes had gone hand-in-hand. Of the twenty-three indicted, eleven pleaded guilty, ten were convicted, and the remaining two were convicted in separate cases. Sentences ranging from twenty to one hundred years were imposed.

It became clear during the trials that the brotherhood of hate is united. Klansmen, Skinheads, neo-Nazis all perceive the same enemies: foreigners, blacks, Jews. They differ only on tactics, and even there the differences are relatively meaningless. Those who do not advocate revolution sympathize with those who do. Old-line Klansmen and Skinheads demonstrated in support of the CSA defendants; Tom Metzger, one-time Grand Dragon and political aspirant, attended The Order trial and denounced the verdict, declaring that the jury had created "ten martyrs."

These were "martyrs" without a following. The prosecutions had virtually wiped out the Klan as a national force. Three major Klans in the 1970s had had members in many states. Today these Klans—the United Klans of America, the Knights of the Ku Klux Klan, and the Invisible Empire, Knights of the Ku Klux Klan—have been reduced to skeletons. They have members mainly in isolated pockets in the South.

This does not mean that there has been an end to violence. The Klan, in areas where it still has cells, indulges as always in racial intimidation: in beatings, the burning of crosses, the desecration of synagogues, the trashing of black homes. Indeed, it seems at times as if the weakening of the major Klans has increased the frustration and frenzy of the die-hard members who are left.

In 1983, in retaliation for the KLANWATCH suit that had ended the harassment of Vietnamese fishermen in Galveston, the Klan fire-bombed and destroyed the Montgomery, Alabama, offices of the Southern Poverty Law Center. Three Klansmen were arrested and convicted for the deed.

But Klan hatred and a desire for vengeance still hang heavy over the law center and its chief counsel, Morris Dees. Klansmen have vowed to kill Dees, whose successful suits have almost bankrupted various Klans and have led to criminal prosecutions. The FBI has notified Dees about these threats and warned him to take them seriously.

Just as the older Klans thrash around in venemous rage, so do the new recruits to racial hate, the militant Skinheads. Not all Skinheads are racist. Nonracist Skinheads held a rally in Minneapolis, Minnesota, in early 1989 to protest the damage done to their image. They appeared, however, to represent only a small minority in the Skinhead movement.

Racist Skinheads have been far more visible across the nation. KLANWATCH data show that these Skinheads, in addition to three murders, committed half the assaults motivated by racial, religious or ethnic bias during the first half of 1988.

In San Diego, California, three Skinheads were convicted for assaulting two Vietnamese with a deadly weapon. In Spokane, Washington, two Skinheads were arrested for knifing a black man while he waited for his girl friend in a grocery store parking lot. In Milwaukee, Wisconsin, two Skinheads were arrested for shooting and wounding a youth as he drove in a car past the home in which they lived. Other Skinheads had been arrested in four cases of battery or disorderly conduct within two months. In Mariposa, California, three Skinheads, brandishing firearms, were arrested after they attacked black families who were camping in a public park. In Westminster, California, an integrated town just east of Huntington Beach, Skinheads paraded through the streets, shouting, "White power! White power!" A cross was burned, several homes were vandalized, and a large rock with an attached note threatening Asians was hurled through the window of a liquor store owned by a man of Korean descent. In Kenosha, Wisconsin, two Skinheads were arrested for firing shots through the windows of an all-black church where a Bible group was meeting. The list goes on and on.

The Skinheads who commit such hate-motivated crimes are for the most part poorly educated and ignorant and feel short-changed by society. A Jacksonville, Florida, detective who questioned several of them after they were arrested in a violent street demonstration drew an unflattering picture. He said they "were able to recite their basic right-wing philosophy, but they were unable to give a single argument in support of their cause. And they had no concept of history, and didn't understand why wearing a swastika on your shirt would be offensive to some people."

Such youths are much like their older Klan mentors, who were perhaps best described by William Sullivan, once the number two man in the FBI. He wrote in his memoir that he had seen the Klan in action when he was a boy in Massachusetts and that they had seemed "like hoodlums" to him then. And he added: "I never learned anything about them to cause me to change my opinion."

BIBLIOGRAPHY

Anti-Defamation League of B'nai B'rith. *Facts. 25:3* (1979)

Bowers, Claude G. *The Tragic Era.* Boston: Houghton Mifflin, 1929

Chalmers, David M. *Hooded Americanism: The First Century of the Ku Klux Klan, 1865-1965.* New York: Doubleday, 1965.

Doar, John, and Dorothy Landsberg. "The Performance of the FBI in Investigating Violations of Federal Laws Protecting the Right to Vote, 1960-1967." Paper delivered at Princeton University, October, 1971.

Jackson, Kenneth T. *The Ku Klux Klan in the City, 1915-1930.* New York: Oxford University Press, 1967.

Lytle, Andrew Nelson. *Bedford Forrest and His Critter Company.* New York: Minton, Balch, 1931.

Robbins, Peggy. "Louisiana Lottery Was So Big It Didn't *Have* to Be Rigged." *Smithsonian Magazine* (1979).

Rowe, Gary Thomas. *My Undercover Years with the Ku Klux Klan.* New York: Bantam, 1976.

Roy, Ralph Lord. *Apostles of Discord.* Boston: Beacon Press, 1953.

Sims, Patsy. *The Klan.* New York: Stein & Day, 1978.

Sullivan, William C., with Bill Brown. *The Bureau: My Thirty Years in Hoover's FBI.* New York: W.W. Norton, 1979.

Thompson, Charles Willis. *The Fiery Epoch, 1830-1877.* Indianapolis: Bobbs-Merrill, 1931.

Trelease, Allen W. *White Terror: The Ku Klux Klan Conspiracy and Southern Reconstruction.* New York: Harper & Row, 1971.

Whitehead, Don. *Attack on Terror.* New York: Funk & Wagnalls, 1970.

____.*The FBI.* New York: Pocket Books, 1956.

KLANWATCH publication of the Southern Poverty Law Center, Montgomery, Alabama, files for the years 1980–1988.

The Monitor, publication of the Center for Democratic Renewal, Atlanta, Georgia, issues for 1987 and 1988.

Newsweek, February 23 and September 7, 1987.

New York Daily News, October 31 and November 4, 1988.

The New York Times, October 26 and December 31, 1988.

The New York Times Magazine, November 1, 1987.

INDEX

ABOUT THE AUTHOR

Fred J. Cook is the author of more than thirty books. A Phi Beta Kappa journalism graduate of Rutgers University, he worked as a journalist for a number of years before becoming a freelance writer. He has written several hundred magazine articles, published in *The Nation, The New York Times Magazine, Saturday Review,* and *American Heritage.* Mr. Cook has won four Page One Awards from the Newspaper Guild of New York and a Sidney Hillman Foundation prize for the best magazine article of the year. His books include *The FBI Nobody Knows, The Muckrakers,* and *Nightmare Decade.*